CW00493129

A QUICK GUIDE TO FREEMASONRY

David Harrison

Lewis Masonic

*This book is dedicated to new
Freemasons everywhere*

First published 2013

ISBN 978 0 85318 440 9

© David Harrison 2013

Published by Lewis Masonic

an imprint of Ian Allan Publishing Ltd, Hersham, Surrey KT12 4RG.

Printed in England

Visit the Lewis Masonic website at www.lewismasonic.co.uk

Distributed in the United States of America and Canada by BookMasters
Distribution Services.

FRONT COVER *Duke of Sussex's Grand Master's Jewel © Library & Museum
of Freemasonry, London.*

All photographs are copyright the author unless stated.

Contents

Abbreviations

AQC	Transactions of the Ars Quatuor Coronatorum
JCRFF	The Journal for the Centre of Research into Freemasonry and Fraternalism
JIVR	The Journal of the Institute of Volunteering Research
THSLC	Transactions of the Historic Society of Lancashire and Cheshire
UGLE	The United Grand Lodge of England

Acknowledgements

In the writing of this book I would like to thank Martin Faulks for giving me the idea, the concept and the outline of the book; Pip Faulks for the editing and advice; Dr Gary Lock for the excellent accommodation in London; Helen Kendrick, and friends and family for their support. I would also like to thank David Moran, David Cook, Alan Bevins and David Lauretti for their advice on lodges in the USA, Australia, New Zealand and Canada respectively, Kenneth Jack for his information on Scottish lodges, Stephen Jordan of Acacia Masonic for supplying me with the 'Humber Use' ritual book, Jim MacDade for the many other ritual books, John Soderblom and Daniel Killpartrick of the North Reading Lodge in Massachusetts, USA, Alec Gerard of the Merchants Lodge, Vic Charlesworth at the Warrington Masonic Museum, and many other Masons who gave me their time and supplied information on ritual working over the years – you know who you are.

Foreword by Martin Faulks

It is with great pleasure that I write the Foreword for David Harrison's latest work, *A Quick Guide to Freemasonry*. I say *pleasure*, because I love Freemasonry. Freemasonry and its goals are in line with my own interests and goals in life. Primarily, Freemasonry is about the cultivation of virtue and noble acts. In my life Freemasonry holds a place like that of an extremely inspiring play, but also of a tradition which contains the wisdom of many centuries of human endeavour. Before one joins Freemasonry, it is extremely hard to understand the brotherhood Masons share and the support that it brings to the life of someone initiated into our Order. The social side of Freemasonry is something that I'll always value. I find myself intellectually stimulated and inspired in the temple and full of joy and celebration at the Festive Board.

For this reason, I would always support anything which supports Freemasonry and Freemasons. It is for that very reason that I chose to work for Lewis Masonic. Lewis Masonic was founded in order to help Freemasonry, the same way that a Lewis lifts a stone or the way that the son of a Mason is supposed to support his father. This book really does that.

It supports Freemasonry in many ways - a simple layout, the knowledge contained, and its focus not only on the basic information but also the interesting and often unknown facts. Because of its question-and-answer format, it makes a great introduction for both the non-Mason and the new initiate. It is also easy just to dip in and out for people who are extremely busy. For that reason, it will be highly popular with experienced Masons.

The simple Q&A format makes it suitable for Masonic units, Lodges, or organisations to use as part of their education program. It's so easy just to have a question and, of course, the answer, read out at the beginning or the end of a meeting. This way, Freemasons are continuing to make a daily advancement in their Masonic knowledge. I also believe that the book could be used for fund-raising purposes – such as a Lodge quiz night held for charity.

In this book, you have a ready-made set of questions and answers on all the basic information about Freemasonry as well as more in-depth subjects to help Brethren find both something interesting and new contained within. It is for this reason that I believe that this book reflects both the aims of Freemasonry and the aims of its brethren in general. Very few titles help our moral education, bring inspiration and help charity. This handy book fulfils all three purposes.

Introduction

When I became a Freemason way back in 1998, I was confused and totally mesmerised by what had just happened; the initiation ceremony was dramatic, mystifying and left me with more questions than answers. After an experience like that it makes you aware that you have just partaken in an ancient rite of passage; a ceremony that reflects age-old aspects of a traditional initiation into ancient mysteries. The initiation ceremony reminded me of something that is embedded in the human character, something rooted very deep in human emotion – the essence of trust in ones fellow man (and woman), bonding, brotherhood and sisterhood.

The initiation ceremony was a whirlwind of an experience and at first I couldn't make sense of it and was full of questions; where did it originate? Why roll your trouser leg up? Filled with these questions, and many more, I turned to the Internet which led me to conspiracy websites and half-truths rather than official answers. The lodge was mainly filled with older men who wouldn't answer my questions, saying that it would spoil the experience of the next degree ceremony. There were no official mentors in the lodge at this time, everyone was busy doing their own particular role, and my original questions, some of which appear in this book, I have found to be repeated by new members all the time, Freemasonry being as perplexing to them now as it was to me then; why does it need seven Masons to open a lodge? Why do Freemasons use the colour blue on their aprons? Why are there so many variations of the ritual? Why do we toast so many people I have never heard of at the festive board?

Of course, every lodge is different, and lodges in other countries are very different – making Freemasonry very confusing to new initiates. Entering into Craft or Blue lodges for the first time is such an overwhelming experience that it is sometimes very hard to take it all in. And on top of that, Freemasonry is a very personal experience, everyone you ask has a different opinion; you can ask many 'expert' Freemasons the same question and get many differing answers. So this guide book is a *quick guide book*, it is an attempt for me to answer questions regarding Craft or Blue Freemasonry that I wanted to ask when I was initiated, in an easy to understand fashion. This book also represents questions that have been submitted to me by new Freemasons and people who are merely interested in Freemasonry, both male and female, so these are your answers, written informally but with references and a bibliography, which gives an option for further reading.

My answers come from my own personal experiences within Freemasonry, from visiting many lodges; old lodges and new lodges, and from talking to numerous Freemasons; old Masons and new Masons. A multitude of sources have been used; from exposés of the ritual from the eighteenth and nineteenth centuries, various editions of the *Book of Constitutions*, lodge histories, and many books that have been published on Freemasonry, as well as the advice of fellow Freemasons.

Sometimes there is never a straight answer; sometimes the explanation goes on for quite a while before the final door is opened to reveal something even more complex - a riddle inside an enigma, which in itself leads to more questions. Indeed, this is all part of the Masonic journey, and I hope this small book, which has been designed for new Freemasons, to be reader friendly and easy to use, will be a small step on your own part of that journey.

Dr David Harrison
Master Mason

FAQs

What is Freemasonry?

Freemasonry is a society that produces a different meaning for different people; for some, it provides an insight into the hidden mysteries of nature and science, for others it provides an opportunity to meet like-minded people; it creates social events for its members, and it gives an opportunity to give something back to society as a whole in the form of charity. For others, it is merely a hobby. We will later examine in more detail what Freemasonry means to certain members, and the type of gentlemen the society attracted, such as the many Fellows of the Royal Society.

Can anyone join Freemasonry?

Any male of good character can join, generally at the age of 21, though as we shall see, there are certain lodges that allow candidates at the age of 18. There is Freemasonry for women, and there is also Co-Masonic organisations, which allow both men and women to join. This will be explored in more detail later.

What is meant by the terms 'Operative' and 'Speculative' Mason?

'Operative' Masons are Masons who actually work in stone, whereas 'speculative' Masons are Masons who use the working tools, the working processes and the symbols of the 'operative'

Masons, in a moralistic way. For example, the working tools of the 'operative' Mason are revealed to have moralistic features, the working processes of the 'operative' Mason are revealed within the progressive journey of the candidate – first as an Entered Apprentice, Fellowcraft then as a Master Mason, and the many symbols used by 'operative' Masons as stonemasons marks – the square and compass' for instance, all hold moralistic properties.[1]

A medieval scene showing a stone mason and carpenter.

What do the 'rough' and 'smooth' ashlars represent?

The rough and smooth ashlars represent the progressive educational journey of Mason; from Entered Apprentice,

Fellowcraft, and finally as a Master Mason, the Mason learns how to smooth and perfect the ashlar, his craftsmanship and education developing to acquire the skills needed to prepare the dressed stone for use in building. Of course, we, as Speculative Masons, look at the rough and smooth ashlars in a moralistic sense, and by the use of the working tools, which are presented as the Mason progresses from Entered Apprentice to Master Mason, the Mason can attain moralistic and spiritual perfection, the Mason becoming more refined and perfected.

What is the Masonic letter 'G'?

The letter 'G' appears on the ceiling of most lodges in England, and in the second degree, we learn that the letter is *'denoting God - the Grand Geometrician of the Universe, to whom we must all submit and whom we ought humbly to adore'*.[2] In the USA, it is common for the letter 'G' to appear behind the Worshipful Master's chair. The letter 'G' is of course the seventh letter of the English alphabet, seven being an important number in Freemasonry. In the Hebrew alphabet, it is called *'Gimel'* and occupies the third place, three being an important Masonic number.[3]

Which Charities do the Freemasons give money to? Is it just Masonic causes?

There are many different charities that Freemasons give to; it could be in support of local causes such as restoring a church roof, helping a local hospice or it could be in support of the many Masonic charities, such as the Masonic Schools for girls and for boys, and the Masonic Samaritan fund. Charity and education always featured heavily within Freemasonry, with local lodges and individual Masons during the eighteenth and nineteenth century contributing towards the building of local schools, colleges and churches. In 1933, the Royal Masonic Hospital in London was opened by King George V, its building being made possible by the contribution of Freemasons throughout England, and during the eighteenth and early nineteenth centuries, local lodges had burial or sickness funds. This 'benevolent' feature of Freemasonry will be explored later.[4]

Where does Freemasonry come from?

Freemasonry has developed from the medieval Mason's Guilds, which began to allow an influx of non-operative members during the early seventeenth century. It began to develop its administration, forming a Grand Lodge, revising its rituals and ceremonies, until it transformed into the society it is today.

When was the first Grand Lodge formed?

The first Grand Lodge was founded in London on the 24th of June, 1717, meeting in the Goose and Gridiron Ale House and was thus termed the 'Premier' Grand Lodge. Certain

Masonic historians have put forward that the York Grand Lodge was operating as a Grand Lodge before London, but even though they had an administration working and met to elect Presidents to reside over their local body, they did not actually term themselves as a Grand Lodge with Grand Masters, until December 1725.[5]

How many Freemasons are there?

According to the website of the UGLE, there are over 250,000 under the UGLE, and under the Grand Lodge of Scotland and the Grand Lodge of Ireland combined there are an estimated 150,000. Worldwide there are approximately six million Freemasons.[6]

How many degrees are there?

There are three Craft degrees; that of Entered Apprentice, Fellowcraft and Master Mason. These three degrees display a rite of passage set within a moral story, something that will be explained in more depth later. The Royal Arch under the UGLE is considered to be the completion of the Third Degree, although this was not always the case; under the 'Antient' Grand Lodge, the York Grand Lodge and the Wigan Grand Lodge, it was considered a fourth degree in its own right. Other side-degrees, or side-Orders, are under separate administrative bodies, such as Mark Masonry, Knights Templar, and the Red Cross of Constantine, and continue to explore the themes of Freemasonry.

Who was the first Grand Master?

The first ever Grand Master of the English 'Premier' Grand Lodge was Anthony Sayer, installed in June, 1717. Sayer was a bookseller based in Covent Garden, though he was later described as a 'gentleman' in the *Constitutions*.[7]

What is a Lewis?

A 'Lewis' is a son of a Freemason, and, in certain jurisdictions, still has the privilege of being able to be initiated at the age of 18, as opposed to the age of 21 which is the usual age when one can become a Freemason.[8] There is also the Lewis lifting device which is on display in certain lodges; an operative device designed to lift heavy stone into its place. The Lewis device was used as early as the Roman period, the origin of the name is somewhat obscure, though may come from the Latin *levo*. There are many different types of Lewis, such as the External Lewis and Dovetailed Lewis. Within Freemasonry, the Lewis device denotes strength.

What is a Cowan?

A Cowan is an intruder or eavesdropper to Freemasonry, and is an older linguistic term for a rough builder who was not trained in the craft of stonemasonry, akin to someone who constructed dry stone walls as opposed to a stonemason who served his apprenticeship and constructed fine buildings such as Cathedrals and

Churches. An early appearance of the term Cowan is in the Scottish Schaw Statutes, which dates from 1598, and says '*That no Master or Fellow of Craft receive any cowans to work in his society or company, nor send none of his servants to work with cowans.*'[9] An early English mention can be seen in the 1738 edition of Dr James Anderson's *Constitutions*, where it says '*But Free and Accepted Masons shall not allow cowans to work with them...*' indicating that Cowans were considered to be not skilled in the art and were thus treated as inferior.[10]

In the current ritual, the Junior Warden describes part of the duty of the Tyler '*keep off all intruders and cowans to Masonry...*'[11] so even today, a Cowan is seen as an imposter and should not be allowed in a lodge, where he could discover the secrets of Freemasonry.

Why do initiates have to roll their trouser leg up?

The rolling up of the trouser leg is perhaps the most famous image of a Freemason to non-Masons, and there have been many bizarre reasons given for this by various writers: some examples include—to look for a shackle or shackle mark on the ankle to see if the initiate is indeed a 'free man', or to see if there is hair on the leg to prove the initiate is of mature age, the list is endless. In the 18th century however, when knee breaches were fashionable, it was the stocking

that was actually rolled down, and this can be seen by many as a sign of humility, but the central part of this symbolic act is that the actual knee of the initiate is bare. The initiate is asked to kneel to take his obligation, which is taken on the sacred book of the initiates' own religion, be it the Bible, *Quran*, etc., and with the knee being bare, there is respect of the holy ground that the initiate is kneeling on.

The Ceremony of Introducing a Intended Brother into the Lodge

A print taken from a rare 1769 edition of the *Constitutions*, revealing an initiation ceremony, with the candidate's stocking rolled down and his knee length breeches pulled up slightly to reveal the knee. Notice the drawn swords. This particular edition of the *Constitutions* is held by the Warrington Masonic Museum.

Why do Freemasons wear white gloves?

The white gloves of a Freemason represent purity, and, like the apron, are symbolic in nature, reflecting how the medieval stonemasons wore gloves during their work to protect their hands. Some lodges and jurisdictions allow symbols on the gloves; other lodges prefer their gloves to be purely white. White kid gloves were once used, but now the gloves generally worn by Freemasons are white cloth. It also looks rather striking with the white gloves and dark clothing that most lodges under the United Grand Lodge of England wear, reflecting the black and white chequered flooring. The first record of a Freemason wearing white gloves in the lodge room occurs on 15th January, 1599, in the records of the Kilwinning Lodge in Ayrshire, Scotland, which state that Donald Ian Fraser, upon his initiation, was presented with a pair of white gloves by his fellow Masons to commemorate the occasion.

From the 1720s, records refer to the custom of the initiate himself presenting a pair of white gloves to each of the brethren who attended his initiation. However, by the mid eighteenth century, in many lodges, this was altered to the initiate then being presented with two sets of white gloves; one pair for his own use, and the other a pair of longer gloves, for the lady of his choice. Whilst these two particular customs are still practiced in certain continental lodges, English lodges have reverted to the traditional custom of presenting a pair of white gloves to the initiate.

Why do Freemasons wear aprons?

Freemasons wear aprons to symbolise the protective work aprons worn by the medieval stonemasons. The white lambskin aprons worn by the initiate symbolise purity and innocence. The investiture of the white apron goes hand in hand with investiture of the white gloves, though in some jurisdictions, symbols are allowed on the gloves. After the Second Degree, a Fellowcraft apron is presented to the candidate, which features a badge, making fellow Masons aware of his position within Freemasonry. Only when he has completed the Third Degree is a Master Mason's apron presented, the light blue of the apron again indicating his status.[12]

Is Freemasonry a religion?

Freemasonry is not a religion, but it has obvious religious overtones; the Third Degree ritual having hints of older, Christian references, the ritual also has tinges of Judaism scattered throughout, with obvious references to the Old Testament, especially with the ritual alluding to Solomon's Temple and King David, and the ritual is embedded with esoteric meaning, such as the necromantic imagery displayed in the Third Degree.

Freemasonry provides a personal experience, and for some, it provides a spiritual dimension. The ritual can be a moving experience, and being littered with poetical devices and religious references, it invokes feelings of spirituality. After all, the lodge is a sacred space where religion is not allowed to be discussed, bringing men and women, from all religious backgrounds together in harmony.

How Many Masons does it take to open a lodge and why?

It takes seven Masons to open a lodge; the Worshipful Master, the Senior and Junior Wardens, the Senior and Junior Deacons, the Inner Guard and Tyler. With these Officers, a lodge can be tiled and opened, and this is represented in the old Masonic symbol of the beehive, which could be seen with seven bees around it. Seven is also a prime number, and an important number within Freemasonry.

Would I really suffer having my throat cut across, tongue torn out by the root, and my body buried in the rough sands of the sea, if I revealed any secrets of Freemasonry?

No, the dramatic penalties described in the first-degree ritual are powerful symbolic images representing the punishment of betrayal to a trusted brotherhood. The secrets of Freemasonry have been in the public

domain for centuries, with the first of a number of exposés being published in 1730. Radical writers such as Thomas Paine and Richard Carlile also published essays and exposés on the ritual, and all died a natural death.

William Morgan however, who wrote an exposé entitled *Illustrations of Masonry* which was published in the US in 1827, mysteriously disappeared before the work was published, and a number of Freemasons were charged with his kidnapping. Morgan's disappearance and the intrigue surrounding the affair caused a public backlash against Freemasons in New York and neighbouring states, and the Anti-Masonic Political Party was founded, which ran a candidate opposing the Freemason Andrew Jackson in the 1828 election. Freemasonry was openly criticised as a result and many lodges in the New York area endured low membership with some lodges closing. The English radical writer Richard Carlile who had published his own exposé slightly earlier, claimed to be an influence on Morgan's work, and sensationally stated that Morgan had been murdered by Masons; a theory that had quickly took hold soon after Morgan's disappearance and fuelled anti-Masonic opinions.[13]

So what real penalties exist?

Suspension and expulsion have been the penalties for the likes of creating disputes and disturbances in the lodge room, amongst other dishonorable actions, such as fraud. Even the Grand Lodge of Wigan expelled one of their Grand Secretaries for fraudulently embezzling Grand Lodge funds in 1824![14]

During the eighteenth and nineteenth centuries, there certainly seems to have been far more alcohol consumed during lodge meetings (though some existing brethren would argue that point), and there are many lodge minutes, which tell of drunken arguments and heated incidents during meetings, such as the Lodge of Lights in Warrington, Lancashire, where there were a lot of fines for drunkenness, swearing, and general raucous behaviour:

In July 1797:

'Mr. Samuel Barrow of Burtonwood was initiated into the first degree of Masonry. He was much intoxicated and counselled to come no more in that condition.'[15]

In May 1798, two brethren were again charged for the use of improper and insulting language, and the drunkenness of the brethren was again evident during the September meeting in 1801. The misuse of drink was apparent again in the March of 1803 when:

'Bro. Holmes, who had been initiated three years before, took the chair because the W.M. came intoxicated - the W.M. was suspended till May.'[16]

The drunken behaviour continued in the September of 1804, when, a certain *'Bro. John Hamlett'* was fined for entering the lodge intoxicated, and in 1806, Joseph Leather was forever expelled from the lodge for his ever-increasing drunkenness and offensive behaviour.[17]

So does being a Freemason really brings perks, such as if you are stopped for speeding, a Masonic nod and a wink will get you off?

Officially, there are no perks like that at all. There are certainly police officers who are members of Freemasonry, and Stephen Knight wrote about this subject (and perhaps accelerated the myth of this type of behavior), in his book *The Brotherhood*, which caused a media sensation when first published in the early 1980s. The book abounds with stories of the police and judges in the UK perverting the course of justice by using their Masonic connections, but Knight does not reveal the sources for his information.[18] It was the belief in this supposed behaviour of 'favour swapping' and the suspicion surrounding the secrecy of Freemasonry, which, as one time Home Secretary Jack Straw once put forward, may create *'a lack of impartiality or objectivity'* that led to the attempt by Straw to pass laws suggesting that Freemasons who join the police or judiciary would have to declare their membership. There was however, no change in the law in England.[19]

Why can't women join Freemasonry?

Freemasonry, under the United Grand Lodge of England, and indeed under the many State Grand Lodges in the US, and the Grand Lodges of Australia and New Zealand, do not permit women as members. Freemasonry emerged from a male dominated society during the seventeenth and eighteenth centuries, a society, which also witnessed the development of the many gentlemen's clubs, a by-gone age when men dominated business, trade and politics. Freemasonry was thus a male only society. There are however historical incidences of women being apprenticed to stonemasons, and occasionally entering lodges. There are various sources, such as in the exposé *Jachin and Boaz*, published in 1762, which refer to a lodge in Ireland that admitted a woman during that period, the anonymous author of the work stating that she was '*as good a Mason as any of them*'.[20]

Society has thankfully changed, but, like Freemasonry under the UGLE, some of the gentlemen's clubs still do not accept women.[21] There is Co-Freemasonry, which accepts both sexes, and women now have their own independent Masonic Order. In France during the late eighteenth century, when, the Grand Orient de France allowed what was termed the 'Rites of Adoption' – lodges being able to accept women, conveying to them the mysteries of the Order. It was not until the later nineteenth century that the first Grand Lodge of Co-Freemasonry was founded, which ultimately led to Freemasonry for both men and women spreading to the UK and the USA, and today a number of 'Co-Masonic' Orders exist.

Of course, the wives of Freemasons do play an important role in the organisation of the social events of lodges, such as the Ladies Evening events and dinner dances that occur. The charitable events of many lodges rely heavily on the support and participation of the wives and family of Masons, and without whom much of the fund-raising and social events would not take place.[22]

Can people with disabilities join the Freemasons?

People with disabilities can join and enjoy Freemasonry. It does state in the Emulation Ritual during the First Degree that the candidate should be '*fit*',[23] and in the *Book of Constitutions*, it states in number IV of the *Ancient Charges*, that the candidate must have '*no maim or defect in his body that may render him incapable of learning the art*',[24] though the use of these expressions within Freemasonry come from a past which could discriminate against disability, and, in regards to the Ancient Charge, it is descended from the actual Ancient Charges compiled by Dr James Anderson in 1723, which were taken from medieval sources. So, today these are merely symbolic of the rules adhered to by the medieval stonemasons.

The Masonic Halls and pubs that house the lodges that I have been to in recent years all have had facilities for disabled brethren; facilities such as wheelchair ramps, lifts, stair lifts, and disabled parking. There are of course a large number of elderly brethren who still attend lodges, many of whom still enjoy the ritual and the work of the lodge, despite feeling the limitations that the onset of age can bring.

In regards to brethren with hearing loss, there is an Order based in the US called the Order of Desoms, which is a lodge that assists Masons who are hard of hearing, and there are Braille editions of ritual books for partially sighted or blind Masons.

Can you become a Mason younger than the age of 21?

Yes, the University lodges, such as the lodges attached to the Universities of Oxford and Cambridge, can admit candidates from the age of 18. These were the two original lodges attached to Universities; the Isaac Newton University Lodge No. 859, which was open to students and graduates of Cambridge University, and the equivalent lodge for Oxford University students and graduates called the Apollo University Lodge No. 357. The Apollo University Lodge first met in 1819, and boasts the past membership of Oscar Wilde, Cecil Rhodes, along with the membership of Royal brethren such as Albert Edward, Prince of Wales who was Worshipful Master

in 1873 and Prince Leopold who served as Worshipful Master in 1876; both being members while they were students at Oxford University.

The Isaac Newton University Lodge, along with the Oxford based Apollo University Lodge, once publicised that they had the exclusive distinction of accepting members from under the age of 21 on the Provincial Grand Masters' judgment, though other University lodges, such as the University Lodge of Liverpool No. 4274, constituted in 1921, can now, through the UGLE Universities Scheme, which was started at the beginning of 2005, also obtain special dispensations for undergraduates from the age of 18. Other University lodges include the Lodge of Fraternity No. 1418 in Durham, the University Lodge, Sheffield No. 3911. There are over forty lodges attached to the scheme.[25]

Are there political links within Freemasonry in England?

Officially there are no political links within English Freemasonry, or for that matter, with Freemasonry in the US. In England however, we currently have a Royal Grand Master in the Duke of Kent, and all lodges toast the Queen – the head of state of the UK – during the festive board. During the Charge given by the Worshipful Master after initiation, the candidate is asked to never lose sight 'of the allegiance due to the Sovereign of your native land', reminding him of the '*indissoluble attachment towards that country whence you derived your birth and infant nurture.*'[26] The wording of this is perhaps a throwback to events in the eighteenth century; the Jacobite rebellion took place in 1745 and, in 1799, the Unlawful Societies Act was passed during a period of war with France and growing radicalism in England. Fear of revolt and revolution dominated the period, and all societies that included oath taking were targeted. Freemasonry was affected, and managed to survive by each individual lodge having to submit a list of members.[27]

During the nineteenth century, it became common for lodges to celebrate coronations by joining the town's processions, but awareness of the possible political connotations to Freemasonry were apparent, such as when the Friendly Lodge No. 557, based in Barnsley, Yorkshire, decided not to take part in a procession in celebration of William IV in 1831, saying that '*we, as Freemasons cannot with propriety join the public procession to celebrate the King's Coronation… because that ceremony has reference to political matters…*'[28] In the US, many past Presidents have been Freemasons, and this will be discussed later.

Is it an obligation or an oath, which is given in Freemasonry?

Today in Freemasonry it is officially an obligation, which is given during the ritual, but in the medieval period, it was clearly an oath that was given

by the Mason. The Halliwell Manuscript or the Regius Poem as it is sometimes known, has been dated to 1390 by Masonic historians Halliwell-Phillips and A.F.A Woodford, and is considered the earliest surviving example of the Ancient Charges. The document displays a poem of the moral duties of a Mason, and an oath is mentioned as being made:

'*The fourteenth point is full good law*
To him that would be under awe;
A good true oath he must there swear
To his master and his fellows that be there;
He must be steadfast and also true
To all this ordinance, wheresoever he go,
And to his liege lord the king,
To be true to him over all thing.'[29]

However, the word 'obligation' had started to be used by the eighteenth century, and in the exposés of the period, such as *Jachin and Boaz* and *Three Distinct Knocks*, the word 'oath' is given along with the word 'obligation'.[30] The definition of an oath is a solemn declaration or promise naming God, but an obligation is a binding agreement or a contract, in a legal sense.[31] However, in the 'solemn obligation' given by the Candidate in the First Degree in lodges under the UGLE, a 'promise' is given in '*the presence of the Great Architect of the Universe*', which seems more like an oath than a legally binding obligation.[32]

So why did this change happen? In *Jachin and Boaz*, first published in 1762, the obligation is under the bold heading of 'The Oath' and is given by the candidate '*in the presence of Almighty God*', though in a footnote, the anonymous author of the exposé puts forward that '*the form of an oath differs in many lodges*', with other lodges saying '*in the presence of the Great Architect of the Universe*'. However, overall, the wording in today's obligation is remarkably similar to that displayed in the exposé, and it states at the end of the piece, that it was an '*Obligation*'.[33] In *Three Distinct Knocks* (1760), the piece is presented as a '*Solemn Obligation or Oath*' and almost identical wording is used in the section displayed in *Jachin and Boaz*, with the candidate swearing '*in the presence of Almighty God*', and the word '*obligation*' again being used at the end.[34]

So it appears that the words 'obligation' and 'oath' were blurred at this point, and it was only after the Unlawful Societies Act of 1799 that the word 'oath' disappears. The Act, which was passed by a parliament swathed in a climate of fear, with the French Revolution of 1789, the subsequent Bloody Terror, the rise of Napoleon, rebellion in Ireland in 1798, and revolt in Britain's industrial towns. The Tory government of William Pitt the younger, were concerned with radical secret societies that were swearing oaths, and Freemasonry in Britain managed to escape the Act, with lodges submitting a list of members to a magistrate every year.[35] After the union of the 'Moderns' and 'Antients' in 1813, the ritual was de-Christianised, and in the Richard Carlile exposé of 1825, the word 'oath' has gone, leaving the word 'obligation' only, and the candidate firmly takes the obligation '*in the presence of The Great Architect of the Universe*' instead of '*Almighty God*'.[36]

Are there any Christian elements left in Freemasonry?

Officially there are no Christian elements left in Craft Freemasonry, though there are subtle hints embedded within the ritual that remind us that there were Christian references there. Before the de-Christianisation of the Craft after the Union of the 'Antients' and the 'Moderns' in 1813, Freemasons for example celebrated the two festivals of St John in June and in December, and there were symbols, such as the Ark, which referred to obvious Biblical stories.

However, in the Third Degree of the Emulation Ritual, there is a reference to '*The Lord of Life*' who will enable us '*to trample the King of Terrors beneath our feet*', and to raise our eyes to the '*Bright morning star*' which is a reference to Christ, as mentioned in the *Book of Revelation*, 22:16, where Christ is described as '*the bright star of dawn*'.[37] The Third Degree, in raising the Master Mason from the figurative grave, thus alludes to the resurrection, referring to Christ, '*whose rising brings peace and salvation to the faithful and obedient…*'[38]

The manner of Receiving the word from the MASTER

A print taken from the rare 1769 edition of the *Constitutions*, showing the third degree raising ceremony. *Warrington Masonic Museum*

Masonic History

Who was the first Freemason?

Elias Ashmole was the first recorded English 'speculative' Freemason to be initiated into Freemasonry. He was a Royalist soldier during the English Civil War, and joined a lodge in Warrington, Lancashire, in October 1646. However, in his diary, he mentions that there were other members of the lodge who were not 'operative' Masons (though there was one recorded 'operative' Mason mentioned as being present), so he certainly was not the first, though he can claim to be the first recorded 'speculative' English initiate, although he was joined by another initiate on the same day; Colonel Henry Mainwaring, who was a Parliamentarian during the Civil War.

Where and when was the first Masonic lodge?

These are the two most frequently asked questions, a set of related questions that Masonic historians have tried to answer since Masonic research began! I can only give my theory, which is that 'operative' Masonry—the guilds of the medieval period—formed 'lodges' to organise themselves in certain cities like York, Chester, Edinburgh, London, and in towns such as Warrington. These lodges had their own local traditions, and in the case of the Warrington lodge, had links to operative Masons that worked in sandstone and had access to the *Old Charges*, a set of moralistic guidelines for

Masons. Sometime in the seventeenth century, these 'operative' lodges began to admit 'speculative' members, and when Elias Ashmole was made a Freemason in October 1646, the Warrington lodge could come together after copying the *Old Charges*, especially to admit him.[39]

As previously stated, Ashmole and Henry Mainwaring, who accompanied him into the lodge, were the earliest known English 'speculative' Freemasons to be recorded as being admitted; they were not 'operative', but joined the lodge out of reasons of interest, and there was already a number of local gentlemen involved in the lodge – all 'speculative', and one confirmed 'operative' Mason, hinting that this process of transformation had been underway for at least a number of years. By the end of the seventeenth century there is evidence of other 'speculative' Freemasons joining lodges in York and Chester.

In Scotland, there are earlier and more consistent records, for example the Lodge of Edinburgh, which has minutes dating from 1599, and Mother Kilwinning Lodge, which has minutes beginning in 1642. These records also suggest that an influx of 'speculative' masons were joining these once 'operative' lodges by the mid seventeenth century, a period of social upheaval as Britain was experiencing a Civil War. One example being Sir Robert Moray, who entered the Craft in Newcastle on the 20th of May,

1641, by members of the Lodge of Edinburgh, who like Moray, were in the Scottish army. However, the earliest Scottish non-operative or 'speculative' Mason was the Laird of Auchinleck, who was admitted into the Lodge of Edinburgh in June 1600.[40]

They would have practised a different ritual from what we practice, but the process of transformation was underway, so the 'speculative' lodges that exist today can be traced to the early-mid seventeenth century, in both England and Scotland.

Why are there so many Fellows of the Royal Society that are also Freemasons?

The Royal Society was founded in 1661 by a number of Natural Philosophers such Elias Ashmole, Robert Moray, Christopher Wren, all of course were early Freemasons. The Royal Society was dedicated to the pursuit of natural philosophy, with experiments performed, papers published and lectures given, the society being at the forefront of the practice of Newtonian experimental natural philosophy.

Freemasonry was seen as a gentleman's society, which allowed its members to research '*the hidden mysteries of nature and science*', and many lodges, such as the Kings Lodge in London and the Lodge of Lights in Warrington held scientific related lectures. These included many progressive topics, such as the lectures on astronomy given in the Lodge of Lights during the early nineteenth century. Thus the scientifically interested

brethren could pursue their interests in like-minded company, and many Fellows of the Royal Society became involved with Freemasonry in the eighteenth and nineteenth centuries, for example Benjamin Franklin, Joseph Banks, John Senex, Dr Jean Theophilus Desaguliers, and the Duke of Sussex.

Freemasonry certainly promoted natural philosophy, and the ritual is littered with words such as 'meridian', which reflects the work that Desaguliers was conducting during the 1720s. The theme of the search for lost knowledge, a theme, which would have been instantly recognised by natural philosophers, resounds throughout the Masonic ritual, and this would undoubtedly appeal to men such as Edward Jenner and Alexander Fleming.[41]

Are there any connections between the medieval Knights Templar and Freemasonry?

None whatsoever, there are many speculative books published on this, but there has never been anything proven historically.[42] The Knights Templar, or to give their complete name, The Poor Fellow-Soldiers of Christ and of the Temple of Solomon, was a medieval Order established around 1119, which gave protection to pilgrims during the Crusades of the medieval period. The Knights Templar were initially supported by King Baldwin II of Jerusalem, and their headquarters was based at Temple Mount, which was believed to be built on the ruins of the Temple of Solomon, and it was from this location that the Knights took their name. Their emblem was of two knights riding on one horse, which symbolised their poverty, but this poverty did not last for long, as they became a favoured charity; being granted land, money, and businesses by supporters in aid for the fight for the Holy Land. They became an extremely wealthy Order, and had the backing of many noble families and at one time, the pope himself.

The end of the Order came in 1312, when Pope Clement V, influenced by King Philip IV of France, pressed charges against the Templars, dissolving the Order, and burning the Grand Master Jacques de Molay at the stake in 1314 for heresy. The remaining Templars were either pensioned off or were absorbed into the Knights Hospitallers.

The Masonic Knights Templar Order emerged in the mid-late eighteenth century, more in celebration of the romantic and chivalric image of the medieval Knights Templar, best seen in the Jacobite Freemason Chevalier Ramsey's 'Oration' given in 1737, in which he put forward that Freemasonry had links to the Crusades and Chivalric Orders. There is however, no historical connection between the Knights Templar of the Crusades, and the modern Masonic Order.[43]

What is the link between Masonry and the Red Cross of Constantine?

Like the Knights Templar, the Red Cross of Constantine is a Christian Masonic side Order, and is open to Master Masons who have joined the Royal Arch. The Red Cross of Constantine actually originated in the late eighteenth century, and the Order celebrates the tradition of the Roman Emperor Constantine who witnessed a vision of a cross in the sky as he was marching with his army. Constantine became the first Roman Emperor to encourage Christianity, and after seeing the vision of the cross, the tradition puts forward that a number of Christian soldiers in his army came forward and avowed their faith, leading Constantine to direct that they should wear the red cross on their armour, a conclave of the knights of the Order being opened, the members of which becoming the loyal bodyguards of the Emperor. The Grand Imperial Conclave however, was only established in 1865, despite being practiced as a side 'degree' or Order during the later eighteenth century.[44]

Did William Shakespeare have a connection with Freemasonry?

There is no evidence that William Shakespeare was ever linked with Freemasonry, though he often appears on Internet searches as being connected to early Freemasonry, and he has been the subject of various papers regarding possible links and as being an influence on the Masonic ritual itself.[45]

The essence of tragedy in the Masonic ritual may reflect the popularity of theatre during the seventeenth century, the ritual certainly containing elements of the expression of powerful poetical language that the Shakespeare plays commonly convey. There are indeed, certain similar expressions and phrases used in certain Shakespeare plays that appear in the ritual, such as:

Measure for Measure, Act III, Scene II, lines 9-11: '*furr'd with fox and lamb-skins too, to signify that craft, being richer than innocency...*'[46] a reference that reminds us of the lambskin apron symbolising innocence within Freemasonry. In *The Taming of the Shrew*, Act V, Scene I, line 54: '*What, my old, worshipful old master?*'[47] And another example can be found in *Merry Wives of Windsor*, Act IV, Scene V, line 102: '*Now, whence come you?*',[48] which is language reminiscent of the question put to the Junior Warden from the Worshipful Master in the Third Degree opening.

Though there is no evidence for Shakespeare being involved in early Freemasonry, his fellow playwrights and contemporaries wrote poetry and plays that reflected imagery that became associated with Freemasonry, such as Ben Jonson who wrote about the cult of architecture and attended clubs around London,[49] and Christopher Marlow, who wrote about a mysterious raising ritual in his play *Doctor Faustus*.[50]

What is the Quatuor Coronati Lodge?

The London based Quatuor Coronati Lodge No. 2076 was founded in 1884 as a result of a number of Freemasons who wanted to form a lodge dedicated to the

research of all aspects of the history of Freemasonry. The members presented papers on all aspects of Masonic research, which were then published in their annual *Transactions*, of which, Masonic historian R.F. Gould and many others, such as Golden Dawn founders Dr William Wynn Westcott and the Rev. A.F.A. Woodford, contributed to. Both Westcott and Woodford produced highly esoteric themed papers for the first Volume of the *Transactions* published in 1888, Westcott discussing the Kabbalah and Woodford talking about Hermeticism.[51]

Gould also published a paper in the first volume, which echoed his own search for hidden knowledge entitled *English Freemasonry Before the Era of Grand Lodge*.[52] He went on to publish many varied papers in the *Transactions* searching for the origins of Freemasonry, Gould becoming one of the leading Masonic historians during the late Victorian period. Other founders of the Quatuor Coronati Lodge included the writer Sir Walter Besant, the explorer and archaeologist Sir Charles Warren, and George William Speth. Warren was the elected Founding Master of the Quatuor Coronati Lodge No. 2076 in 1884, but due to his departure to Africa, the lodge did not meet until his return at the end of 1885.

On Speth's motion to form a Literary Society under the guidance and protection of the lodge, a Quatuor Coronati Correspondence Circle was created, which promoted the work done by the lodge, and ensured a wider reading of the *Transactions* and an increased attendance within the lodge meetings.[53] The lodge is still going strong and meets at Grand Lodge, Great Queen Street in London.

Does Freemasonry still have benevolent and sick fund features?

Freemasonry, just like other fraternal societies such as the Oddfellows, Druids and Foresters, did have benevolent and sick fund aspects to it, and this can clearly be seen during the first half of the nineteenth century, especially in the industrial towns of the northwest of England, where more working men appear in the lodges, and claims for relief are regularly made for a variety a reasons.

In lodges such as the Lodge of Friendship in Oldham, a number of claims for relief were made by Brethren, such as in 1792, when a Brother was granted 5/- on the grounds that his wife had been ill for some time, and the lodge actually started its own Benevolent Society in 1828, with a sick fund being founded the following year. The Grand Lodge of Wigan founded a funeral fund for its members in 1839 and also had a sick fund, and for a short time a Doctor's services were paid for.[54]

After the advent of the National Health Service in the UK during the post war period, many of the fraternal societies which had benevolent and sick fund features went into decline, but Freemasonry, which was strongly unified

and, by this time, had a more middle class makeup, was experiencing unprecedented growth. Many of the other societies, such as the Foresters, Druids and Oddfellows, had fractured into rival Orders, and had a membership extracted more from the working classes, which could now benefit from the developments of the welfare state.

Freemasonry in England was still very much involved in the welfare of its sick members; with the aforementioned Royal Masonic Hospital, which had been opened by George V in 1933, and today, Freemasonry still has the Masonic Samaritan Fund, which provides healthcare and support for Freemasons and their dependants, and the Masonic Schools for Girls and Boys. Through the Charity Steward, each lodge still takes a role in the welfare of elderly members and their dependants, so the benevolent and sick fund features, though now modernised, are still embedded within Freemasonry.

Has there ever been any duelling by Freemasons, and were there any reprisals for disputes between Freemasons?

Duelling was a popular means of resolving disputes between gentlemen up until the mid-nineteenth century, and some Freemasons, such as the Duke of Wellington,[55] Alexander Pushkin, Albert Pike and Andrew Jackson, have taken part in famous duels. The Duke of Wellington duelled with the Earl of Winchilsea in Battersea-Fields in March

1829, after Winchilsea had written inflammatory remarks about the Iron Duke in the *Standard*, concerning the Duke's views on Catholic emancipation and his apparent political motives, accusing him of having '*insidious designs for the infringement of our liberties, and the introduction of popery into every department of state*'. In response to the remarks, the Duke called for '*that satisfaction for your conduct which a gentleman never refuses to give*', and Winchilsea accepted. The two men met for the duel at the appointed place and time, and the parties took their ground. Winchilsea received the Duke's fire, though was unhurt. Winchilsea then fired his pistol into the air, and discussion followed, the Duke of Wellington accepting a suitable reparation from Winchilsea, along with his '*expression of regret*' concerning what he had written about the Duke, which was to be inserted in an edition of the *Standard*.[56]

The Russian poet and Freemason Alexander Pushkin however, was not so lucky; having fought several duels, he had amassed some experience, but after scandalous rumours had circulated implying his wife was having an affair with her brother-in-law—the dashing French military officer Georges-Charles de Heekeran d'Anthès—accusations flared and a duel took place in 1837, in which Pushkin was shot in the stomach by d'Anthès, and died two days later. Before he died, Pushkin sent a message to d'Anthès, whom he had wounded in

the arm, pardoning him from any wrong doing, though d'Anthès was imprisoned for a brief time afterwards, as duelling was illegal in Russia.[57]

Freemason Albert Pike was also involved in a famous duel with military commander and fellow Freemason John Selden Roane, in 1847, after Pike, in a letter that was published in the *Arkansas Gazette,* had criticised the military commanders for their incompetent leadership at the Battle of Buena Vista during the Mexican War. Roane, who had commanded a force during the battle, took Pike's comments personally, and issued a challenge to Pike who duly accepted, and the duel took place on a sandbank in the Arkansas River, near Fort Smith, Arkansas, USA. Though a number of shots were fired, no one was injured and both men were persuaded to discontinue the duel by their accompanying surgeons. Pike and Roane went on to become good friends.[58]

There were various incidents of duelling between Freemasons in the US, such as in Kentucky in 1812, where a challenge of a duel passed between two Masons, and the bearer of the challenge being tried by his lodge and suspended for a year. The Grand Lodge of Kentucky became involved, and a special committee eventually concluded that it was entirely improper for a Master Mason to challenge or to convey a challenge to another Master Mason, alluding that Masonic Brothers should live together in harmony. Four years later, the Grand Master who had presided over the matter was himself embroiled in a duel with another Mason, which resulted in their suspension, despite the Freemasons in question being reconciled. A violent incident occurred between two famous Freemasons when there was an altercation between future president Andrew Jackson and future Senator Thomas Hart Benton in Nashville, Tennessee, in 1813, resulting in Jackson being injured. Despite the feuding, Jackson and Benton later became friends and political allies. Both Jackson and Benton were seasoned duellists, both having taken part in well-recorded infamous duels.[59]

Another future president Abraham Lincoln was challenged to a duel by Freemason James Shields after Lincoln was accused by him of being the author of several satirical letters that had appeared in the *Sangamo Journal* of Springfield, questioning Shields' honesty, integrity and lack of courage. Shields was a Democrat, and had become State auditor for Illinois, his policies clashing with Lincoln and the Whig party, and the impending duel created ecstatic anticipation within the towns folk of Springfield. Lincoln, as the challenged party, had the privilege of selecting the terms of the duel, and selected cavalry broadswords as his weapons of choice, and gave instructions that a plank, ten feet in length, was to be fixed on its edge, as a secure line between the two men.

Lincoln measured six feet four inches, and towered over Shields, thus armed with a cavalry broadsword, Lincoln had the advantage with a longer reach. Lincoln and Shields met on an island on the Missouri side of the Mississippi River, on 22nd September, 1842, as duelling was illegal in Illinois, but the duel was called off after friends intervened to get Shields to accept Lincoln's explanation.

Although duels were commonplace during the eighteenth and early nineteenth centuries, personal disputes in lodges in England tended not to lead to such drastic action! There are plenty of references in lodge minute books to disputes between Freemasons, such as in the Lodge of Lights, where in 1806, a dispute between John Evans and Joseph Leather resulted in the latter being dismissed from Freemasonry, Leather being noted as quarrelsome and drunk.[60] Another dispute in the Grand Lodge of Wigan during 1846, between Thomas Leigh and James Hart, resulted in the Grand Lodge coming to a decision that both Masons should ask for pardon or be suspended.[61] The Wigan Grand Lodge had actually been formed due to disputes between Freemasons, the ensuing quarrel being personal, bitter and very public, with inflammatory comments being made against both the Grand Master of the United Grand Lodge, the Duke of Sussex, and the antagonistic rebel leader Michael Alexander Gage, though no duel was ever held.

Ritual

Where does the Masonic ritual come from?

The Masonic ritual has changed and transformed over the centuries, and its origins are truly enshrouded in mystery. The first recorded English Freemason, Elias Ashmole, only writes of being 'made a Freemason'[62] but there certainly seems to have been an initiation ceremony of sorts, based on the medieval stonemason's Guilds for young Entered Apprentices and Fellowcrafts. By the time the 'Premier' Grand Lodge was founded in London in 1717 and the first edition of Dr James Anderson's *Charges* were published in 1723, there seems to have been two degrees, but by the 1738 edition, there were clearly three degrees being alluded to. Dr Jean Theophilus Desaguliers and Dr James Anderson seem to have reshaped the degrees of Entered Apprentice and Fellowcraft and created a third Master Mason's degree, forming a Three Degree system which became popular throughout the lodges of England, Scotland, Ireland, America, Australia and the continent.[63]

What changes has the ritual gone through since then?

The ritual in England and Wales was brought into a standardised format after the union of 1813. A Lodge of Reconciliation was set up in an attempt to standardise the many varied rituals that had been worked throughout the country under the Antient and the Modern Grand Lodges. This took many years to implement and had its difficulties; some lodges had to send delegations down to London to learn the new ritual, such as the Lodge of Probity in Halifax, Yorkshire, which sent a number of its brethren to learn the new working, which on their return, they assisted other lodges in Yorkshire to learn.[64]

There was rebellion in Lancashire against the new imposed system and other alterations in administration, and for 90 years there was an independent Grand Lodge of Wigan which continued to practice the 'Antient' ritual; their leading lodge—the Lodge of Sincerity— conducting their ritual in the lodge room around a 16 foot table.[65] On the whole, the transition took place and most other lodges under the United Grand Lodge of England practiced the new ritual, though as a result of the Lancashire rebellion, a regulation change allowed each lodge to regulate their own proceedings, giving each lodge an element of freedom as long as they were '... *consistent with the general laws and regulations of the Craft*', so during the mid-Victorian period onwards, variations of the ritual emerged such as Bottomley and the Humber Working, and a nostalgia developed where certain lodges harked back to before the union, to add what they believed to be older elements to the existing Emulation Ritual creating a varied and creative aspect to individual lodge working.[66]

In the United States, after the American War of Independence, Grand Lodges were established in the various states and unlike the lodges under the UGLE after the Union, lodges were allowed flexibility, so many variations of ritual developed, such as the Ritual of Pennsylvania, and in the nineteenth century, the Preston-Webb ritual. The Scottish Rite developed and became popular, having a Northern and Southern Jurisdiction, and Prince Hall Freemasonry also became established, gaining recognition from the UGLE.[67]

So the Emulation Ritual was an attempt to standardise everything?

Yes, there was a Lodge of Reconciliation formed in 1816, which dealt with the disputes within the ritual, a move that set out to keep both the 'Moderns' and the 'Antients' contented. An Emulation Lodge of Improvement was set up, first meeting in 1823 at Freemasons' Hall in London, enabling the authentic ritual to be practiced and learned accurately, '*without permitting alteration*'. However, even the Emulation Ritual has changed over the years, with more recent changes occurring in the obligation for example, specifically the references to physical penalties, which was to be omitted from 1986.[68]

Why do English and Welsh lodges use Emulation Ritual and why do some lodges have slightly different working?

After the Unification of the 'Moderns' and the 'Antients' in 1813, the ritual was revised and standardised and the result was the Emulation Ritual. However, after the Liverpool Masonic Rebellion in 1823, a rule was changed in the *Constitutions* to allow lodges to adapt slightly from the Emulation Ritual; '... *that the members present at any lodge have an undoubted right to regulate their own proceedings, provided they are consistent with the general laws and regulations of the Craft*'.[69] Thus many lodges work a ritual with a few words changed here and there or perhaps have roles changed during the ceremony. Examples of this can be seen in Liverpool, where some lodges work the Bottomley Ritual, other lodges work the Nigerian Ritual, which was a ritual working that, as the name suggests, came from Nigeria during colonial times. Examples of older ritual working include the Humber, York and Bristol Workings. All of these rituals however, work the three-degree system, and though they have their differences, either in the wording or in the perambulation, familiarities can be recognised.

So just how many other Craft Rituals are there in England?

There are around 50 different Craft rituals or Workings in England, and if you include the working of individual lodges, there are countless variations. In the north of England, we have already mentioned the Bottomley Ritual which is worked by a number of lodges in Liverpool (of which there are variations in different lodges),[70] there is the Humber Use which is worked by a number of lodges in Hull,[71] there is the Nigerian Ritual which is worked in a number of lodges up and down the country, and of course, the York Working, variations of which are used throughout Yorkshire.

In the south of England, different Craft Workings include the West End Ritual, Hill's North London Working (also known as Taylor's Working), the South London Working, the Oxford Ritual, the Sussex Working, and the Bristol Working (of which there are variations in Bristol lodges). There are many more Craft rituals (far too many to list in one paragraph), but the more common ones include Logic, Stability, Universal and Claret's Working.[72] There are also many individual lodge workings that are only associated with one particular lodge, such as the Merchants Lodge No. 241 in Liverpool, which has its own ritual.[73]

From the outside these rituals look like variations of Emulation, with various roles being changed or the odd wording or phrase being added or taken out. In some cases, the perambulation is different, in others certain sections are missed out entirely. However, lodges that work their own ritual are fiercely independent and defensive of their unique ritual working, and it forms part of the particular lodge tradition. Many of these rituals began to be practiced in the mid-Victorian period, and in some cases, such as the Humber Use and Bottomley Ritual, there was a harking back to the older pre-union rituals. In most cases, it does seem that local areas developed their own way of working the ritual during the Victorian era, and formed their own traditional practices.

During this time, it was forbidden to put the Emulation Ritual in print, so perhaps with no way of revising the Emulation Ritual other than word-of-mouth, subtle changes were made over a period of years and the wording in certain sections began to get changed slightly, and over time it became traditional to a certain lodge. When another lodge was founded in the same area, with Masons from the original lodge, then that same traditional way of working the ritual was passed on.[74]

The Emulation Ritual was only officially published in 1969, so by that time there had been quite a few ritual books privately printed, and these books differed slightly from the Emulation Working. George Claret was the first to have an early ritual printed in the 1830s. Claret had attended the Lodge of Reconciliation and his ritual book was based on the Emulation teachings of Peter Gilkes. During the 1880s, the West End, Logic and Oxford rituals were published, and M.M. Taylor's ritual book appeared in 1908. Taylor originally printed it for Henry Hill who was a member of Marylebone Lodge No. 1305, and this became known as Hill's North London Working or Taylor's Working. More recently, an Association was formed to represent the lodges that used Taylor's Working in 1967, and a Taylor's Lodge of Improvement was subsequently held, with a new edition of Taylor's ritual being published. It is very interesting to see the variations of the ritual, and to see the ritual being performed in many different ways, which makes visiting different lodges an entertaining, worthwhile and educational experience.

What different Scottish Craft Rituals are there?

In Scotland, the William Harvey Ritual is popular, a ritual that was born out of concern of the non-Scottish elements that were entering the Scottish ritual. Other Scottish rituals include the Standard Scottish Ritual, which is similar to Harvey's Ritual with a few nuances, the Modern Scottish Ritual, and the MacBride Ritual. Andrew Sommerville MacBride wrote this particular ritual in 1870, and it varies significantly from the Harvey and Standard Rituals, only being used in a few lodges. As in England, there are individual Scottish lodges that have developed their own particular lodge Workings and own traditional practices. These many different rituals in English and Scottish lodges are

however variations on the same theme, and even if the wording and presentation is different, they all tell the same story within the three degrees.[75]

Why can't we read from the ritual book while taking part in the ceremony?

Some lodges do allow the reading of the ritual book while taking part in the ceremony, and this of course can produce a smooth ritual, with no lines being forgotten and no established Masons shouting lines from the side-lines! But the majority of lodges stay with tradition and this can create an excellent ritual to watch, after all, when you go to watch a play, the actors won't be reading their lines from a script.

The learning of the ritual comes from the time in the eighteenth and nineteenth centuries when some of the men who participated in the ceremony may not have been able to read or write, so they would learn it word of mouth from another Brother (perhaps an early version of a lodge mentor), and then recite and practice it verbally. Even for the learned men who were involved in Freemasonry, the ritual book wasn't officially put into print, so to recite it and perform it, like a play, would be the norm. The result would have been a well-revised ritual, with each Mason passing on their parts to the next Mason.

What does *'So Mote it be'* mean?

'*So mote it be*' ends the Masonic prayer, the word 'mote' is derived from the Anglo-Saxon word *motan* meaning 'to be allowed'. It certainly adds to the atmosphere and mysterious nature of the lodge, being a more traditional and archaic linguistic term and in regard to masonry, can be traced back to the Halliwell Manuscript or the Regius Poem, dated to 1390, where it is included towards the end of the document; '*Amen! Amen! So Mote it be!*'[76]

Why do wiccans and other modern magical traditions use similar terms and symbols to those used in Freemasonry?

Many traditions have used similar symbols but more recently some pagan or magical groups, such as the Hermetic Order of the Golden Dawn which can be traced back to 1887, have used Masonic terminology and symbols in their rituals because a few of the founders were Masons and 'borrowed' much of the rituals for their own use.[77]

Lodge Matters

Why is the discussion of politics and religion forbidden in the lodge room?

The discussion of politics and religion is forbidden in the lodge room to preserve the harmony amongst the brethren within the lodge, which in essence is a sacred space. An early example of this can be seen with the earliest mention of English Freemasonry in October 1646, when Elias Ashmole—a Royalist, and Henry Mainwaring—a Parliamentarian, both entered a lodge in Warrington together. Thus Freemasonry is open to all religions and conflict can be avoided retaining the true spirit of brotherly love at all times.

Why are Candidates divested of metals when they first enter the lodge room?

Candidates are divested of all metals as they are supposed to be without money—'*a poor candidate*'[78]—as it is not determined by a man's external wealth whether he is fit for Freemasonry, but by his morals and inner qualities. Being divested of all base metals also means that the Candidate is without the passions and the greed that those base metals can bring. In this sense, there is a link to the alchemists, who were sometimes obsessive in their search for turning base metal into gold. So to be divested of metals is to be divested of the worldly and physical passions, the obsessions, the lust and the greed, without which we are closer to becoming pure.

However, the author Philippa Faulks, who, while researching her excellent book *A Handbook for the Freemason's Wife*, found an issue that seemed to worry some wives of Freemasons, especially in the US. The need for their husbands, as candidates, to remove their wedding rings when, on initiation, they were divested of all metals, led to some of the ladies to be convinced it was a sign that their husbands were being encouraged to be unfaithful!

Why do Master Masons who have never served as Worshipful Master have to leave during installations?

The reason for this could hint at the way the Third Degree was actually created in the early eighteenth century; the term 'master' was originally used as a managerial position, a Master Mason being akin to being a Master of a lodge, so when a Master was installed, the Apprentices and Fellowcrafts who had not served in the position, were not present, as the ceremony was for the installation of the new 'Master'. Indeed, later editions of the Constitutions state that '*In ancient times no brother, however skilled in the craft, was called a master-mason until he had been elected into the chair of a lodge*'.[79]

Thus today, Master Masons (the name now being used to describe the Masons who have been raised to the Third Degree) who have never served as a Worshipful Master, have to leave the

Installation ceremony, as they, like Apprentices and Fellowcrafts, have not, despite their name, yet reached that managerial stage.[80]

What is the difference between an 'alarm' and a 'report'?

This can differ in some lodges, but an 'alarm' is generally considered an 'un-Masonic' knock—a one knock given by the Tyler—to alert the Inner Guard when a Candidate is ready to enter the lodge room at the beginning of a First Degree ceremony. A 'report' is a Masonic knock—when three knocks are given by the Tyler—to alert the Inner Guard, for example when the lodge has opened and a Brother arrives late. The three report knocks differ in rhythm depending on what Craft degree is being worked at the time.[81]

Why do the Senior and Junior Deacons move clockwise in the lodge?

In moving clockwise when escorting the Candidates round the lodge room, the Senior and Junior Deacons look ordered and provide a uniformed, systematic and regulated system of conducting the ceremony. The Deacons also move in a 'clockwise wheel' when conducting the Candidate to turn, but in some Emulation lodges, an anti-clockwise motion is sometimes used.

In some lodges, when entering the lodge room at the start of the meeting, the officers enter in a procession and again, a clockwise format is used; with the Worshipful Master taking his place in the East first, then the Junior Warden takes his place in the South, and finally, the Senior Warden takes his place in the West. A natural progression can then take place in the cycle of the lodge room.

This system is very ordered and also reflects the influence of natural philosophy on Freemasonry; the rhythm and working of the lodge being perfect, disciplined, and professional, so it can quite literally, run like clockwork. The clockwise motion is in contrast to the fact that it was considered unlucky to walk anti-clockwise—or 'widdershins'—around a church, and traditionally, witches walked widdershins while casting spells.

Why do the Senior and Junior Deacons carry wands in the lodge room?

The Senior and Junior Deacons carry wands so they can move freely around the lodge room, and can be relieved from saluting the Worshipful Master and other Officers every time they pass, be it when they carry the minute book for signing (without holding the wand), or when they both conduct the candidates around the lodge room. The wands are also used to point out the steps to be made by the candidate when advancing to the Worshipful Master and Wardens and to point out the seven regular steps in the third degree ritual. The wand is also handed to the Worshipful Master when he is explaining the Tracing Board. The Deacons are the messengers of the lodge, and the rods they carry are symbolic of the *caduceus,* or wand, that the Roman winged god and messenger Mercury carried.

Why is Mercury used as a symbol for the Junior Deacon?

Mercury was the messenger of Jove, known for his speed and mobility, which obviously resounds in the Office of Junior Deacon, and also that of the Senior Deacon; the Junior Deacon carries the messages and communications punctually from the Senior Warden to the Junior Warden, and the Senior Deacon bears the messages and commands from the Worshipful Master to the Senior Warden. Mercury was also a symbol for alchemy, Mercury being able to bring the dead back to life (which reflects the themes portrayed in the Third Degree), and in his possession was an Olive branch wand, which he used to separate two serpents in combat, hence the wand *caduceus* became a symbol of peace, which resounds in the present symbol of the dove and olive branch, used today for the Senior Deacon, and as previously mentioned, in the fact that both Deacons use wands.

In alchemy, an early science, which was researched by early Freemasons Elias Ashmole and Sir Robert Moray, the element of mercury represents movement, fluidity, flux and transformation, and is sometimes known as quicksilver. In ancient China, mercury was thought to be able to prolong life, and the alchemists of the early modern period believed that gold could be produced by varying the

quality and quantity of sulphur contained in the mercury. Another early influential Freemason and natural philosopher Dr Jean Theophilus Desaguliers, was also charged by his patron the Duke of Chandos in 1732, to enquire into the work of the mysterious Baron Silburghe, who had '*found out a secret of fixing quicksilver*'.[82] Mercury was thus extremely important to early alchemists, and early Freemasons, and is very apt that the wands of the two Deacons are symbolic of Mercury, enabling them move freely and promptly in the lodge room to convey messages and to guide the candidates on their Masonic journey, which ends in his rebirth as a Master Mason.

A silver symbol of Mercury holding his staff Caduceus, which was commonly used in many Masonic jurisdictions by the Deacons. After the union in England it was replaced by the symbol of a dove (sometimes carrying an olive branch). This particular silver jewel was made to be attached to a collar of a Deacon, but it was never used as the lodge that had it made was consecrated after the union. *Warrington Masonic Museum.*

Why does the Junior Warden give commands to the Inner Guard and what other traditional duties does the Office hold?

In some jurisdictions, the Junior Warden has the responsibility for examining visiting Freemasons, ensuring that they have the necessary credentials, thus, in England and Wales for example, there is a working relationship between the Junior Warden and Inner Guard in this respect; the Inner Guard is asked by the Junior Warden to see that the lodge is properly tiled, and the Inner Guard alerts the Junior Warden to any visitors arriving. In certain lodges in Ireland, if the Inner Guard is absent, the Junior Warden will also take on his duties.

The Junior Warden, who is '*to call all Brethren from Labour to refreshment and from refreshment to Labour, that profit and pleasure may be the result*', is traditionally charged with supervising the lodge at the festive board or other social events, the Stewards acting as his assistants, and one of his roles is to monitor the amount of alcohol consumed so no Mason succumbs to excess. The symbol of the Office of Junior Warden—the Plumb—reflects this, as it symbolises the upright and moral behaviour of a Mason. As one of the three principal or regular Officers of the lodge, in the absence of both the Worshipful Master and the Senior Warden, the Junior Warden can also take on the responsibilities of the Worshipful Master. It is also a requirement in some jurisdictions, that the Junior Warden is the Officer who is to prefer charges against a Freemason who is guilty of un-Masonic conduct.

Why does the Junior Warden in Freemasonry come from the East?

During the Third Degree opening, the Junior Warden (who is situated in the south of the lodge) is asked by the Worshipful Master '*Whence come you?*' and replies from '*the East*'. The Junior Warden moves from the East to the West to '*seek for that which was lost*', namely '*the genuine secrets of a Master Mason*'.[83] The Junior Warden moves with the Sun, which rises in the East and sets in the West, moving in the southern sky, from the direction of the Worshipful Master, to the Senior Warden. So, in this sense, the East is a place of light, the West a place of darkness, and the journey from East to West is a journey of initiation, a journey of enlightenment; bringing illumination from the East to the West. In the Royal Arch, depending on the ritual variation, a similar question is either put to Haggai or the Principal Sojourner, who answers that he comes from Babylon, and is going to Jerusalem to rebuild the Temple and find the sacred word—Babylon being situated in modern day Iraq, thus he is traveling from the East to Jerusalem in the West.[84]

However, in the 'Humber Use'—a Craft ritual specific to the Hull area in north-east England—the Junior Warden, when asked the same question by the

Worshipful Master, replies he comes from 'The West', which is the complete opposite of the Emulation Ritual, the Liverpool 'Bottomley' ritual, the West End Ritual and most other rituals and individual lodge workings. The Junior Warden is thus moving from the opposite direction to search for what is lost. [85]

The concept of the journey of discovery portraying the prominence of the East and the West can be seen in the 17th degree of the Scottish Rite, called the Knights of the East and West, and the Red Cross of Constantine is described as belonging to the East and West class of initiatory Rites; Constantine becoming the first Roman Emperor to rule from the East in Constantinople, and the West in Rome.

The East is described by Kenneth Mackenzie in his *Royal Masonic Cyclopaedia* as a place that is not only alluding to the rising of the sun, but '*in consequence of our modern civilisation being derived from the Eastern countries.*' The East, with the rising of the Sun, represents the dawn and the awakening, the Junior Warden in the South, allows refreshment at mid-day and the Senior Warden in the West, pays the wages at the close of the day.[86] The journey from the East is thus symbolical; the journey of the Master Mason following the light of the day. The importance of the Sun within Freemasonry in this sense has influenced certain writers, such as Thomas Paine, to put forward how Freemasonry was derived from the Sun worship of the Druids, the ancient journey of initiation resounding in the modern Craft.[87]

Why does the Junior Warden lower his column yet the Senior Warden raises his when the lodge is open?

The column is raised up in the West by the Senior Warden during labour, and placed down in the West at refreshment, whereas the Junior Warden places the column down in the South during labour and raises it up in the South at refreshment. This raising and lowering of the Wardens' columns gives an almost mechanical and ordered action within the working of the lodge, the exquisite attention to detail of the performance of the ritual symbolising the perfection of the lodge working, the actions signifying silently to any entering Brethren the status of the lodge.

The Wardens' columns, or pillars, along with their meanings, made their earliest appearance in 1760, in the exposé *The Three Distinct Knocks*, with the Senior Warden's column being described as '*the strength and support of all business*', and the Junior Warden's column portrayed as '*the Beauty of the day, to call the men off from Work to Refreshment*'.[88] Thus the Senior Warden's column represents Strength, the Junior Warden's column represents Beauty. Another description of the Wardens handling columns appeared in another exposé, *Jachin and Boaz*, published a few years later.[89]

To confuse matters, in some early lodges, the Wardens did not have columns on their pedestals—they had truncheons—perhaps serving a similar function to the truncheons policemen had; to assist in keeping order in the lodge room, albeit in a less aggressive way! An example of this is a lodge in Ireland, which, in the 18th century, had a by-law reading: '*there is to be silence at the first chap of the Master's hamer, and likewise at the first stroke of each Trenchen struck by the Senr and Junr Wardens.*'[90] The nineteenth century Masonic writer Rev. George Oliver also quotes an inventory of a lodge at Chester, England, in 1761, which included '*two truncheons for the Wardens*',[91] and there are still some lodges today, which have truncheons, and not columns, as the symbol of the Wardens. The gavels of the Wardens' may have gradually replaced these truncheons in most lodges, the use of both the gavel and column superseding the elongated truncheon.

Since the Junior Warden's column is raised during refreshment, reason suggests that it would be similarly arranged when the lodge is closed. However, the Wardens' columns are left just as they happen to be placed at the time of closing, except in certain Jurisdictions whose official ritual has ruled a proper positioning of the Wardens' columns at closing.

Why can't Brethren sit in the East of the lodge?

This is to do with Masonic etiquette; Brethren never sit in the East (where the Master sits) without an invitation. All Brethren within the lodge are of course equal, but it is the Master's choice to invite prominent visitors or a special member whom the Master wishes to honour, by sitting with him in the East.

What were the Stewards originally for?

Stewards were appointed to originally serve at the tables during the feasts, bringing the alcohol to the tables, and they still do today. An early Grand Steward was the artist and engraver William Hogarth, who was in attendance serving at a Grand Lodge meeting in 1735.[92]

Is it true that the Tyler used to get paid for Tiling the lodge?

Yes. The Tyler (or Outer Guard) still can get a payment for his duties, which was always seen as an office that involved not only guarding the door, but keeping a record of all the Brethren, checking visitors, drawing the floor of the lodge with chalk and charcoal (complete with the correct symbols for each degree), and holding the keys. The Tyler (or Doorkeeper as the office was referred to) was originally the only office, which didn't require you to be a member of a lodge, or even to be a Freemason; the office sometimes being carried out by the landlord of the tavern where the lodge was held.

There is plenty of evidence in many early lodge minutes, which mentions that the Tyler received a salary, such as the Lodge of Probity in Halifax, which, in the 1760s, records in their cash books that the Tyler was paid one shilling per lodge night for his trouble.[93] Even the Grand Lodge of Wigan paid their Grand Tyler; as in

1845, the Grand Tyler Thomas Green volunteered to give up his salary of twenty shillings (per year) because of the Wigan Grand Lodge debt.[94] Today, the Tyler may still get paid £25-£30 for each meeting.

Is it true that the Entered Apprentices once had to wash the floor of the lodge room after the lodge meeting was over?

Yes, there is evidence that Entered Apprentices washed the floor of the lodge room after the meeting. The floor was drawn before the lodge meeting by use of chalk and charcoal to create the powerful white and black chequered floor of the lodge room—symbolising the light and darkness of human nature, and the necessary symbols. After the meeting was over, the Entered Apprentices were charged with cleaning the floor with a mop and pail. As early as the 1720s, Dr Jean Theophilus Desaguliers put forward that the lodge room should be laid out by the use of tape and nails to introduce a more ordered and precise layout to the lodge.

If there wasn't an Entered Apprentice or other low-ranking Freemason in the lodge, the Tyler would look after the cleaning duties having been charged with the drawing prior to the meeting. In the Royal Arch Chapter, the Tyler's duties are given to the Janitor, who keeps guard outside the Chapter room, and, as the name suggests, one of his duties was to wash off the Chapter floor drawing.

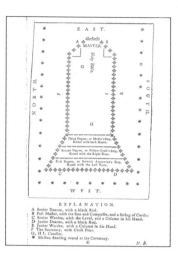

The layout of the lodge room taken from the exposé *Jachin and Boaz*, 1763.

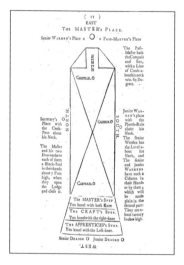

The layout of the lodge room taken from the exposé *Three Distinct Knocks*, 1760. *Both Warrington Masonic Museum*

How do lodges choose their name?

The more modern lodges chose their names upon consecration, such as Domville Lodge which was founded in 1924 and meets in Lymm, Cheshire, which named itself after a local gentry's family. The Authors' Lodge which meets in London and was founded in 1910 was named after the Authors' Club, as a number of its founders were involved in the club. Some lodges have changed their names, such as the De Grey and Rippon Lodge in Liverpool, which was founded in 1871 and originally named after the then Grand Master Earl De Grey and Rippon. After the Earl married a Catholic and resigned from his Office in 1874, the lodge renamed itself Toxteth Lodge.[95] Older lodges founded in the 18th century commonly went by the name of the public house they met at, or their number, but as numbers were changed and more lodges were founded, they began to adopt more personalised lodge names. The Lodge of Probity, consecrated in 1738, and which still meets in Halifax, Yorkshire, chose to name itself after one of its chairs, which still exists. The Royal Lodge of Faith and Friendship, which meets in Berkeley, Gloucestershire, became a Royal lodge after being visited by the Prince of Wales, later George IV. In the United States, lodges have been named after such prominent Freemasons as George Washington or Benjamin Franklin.

Three chairs that belong to the Lodge of Probity, based in Halifax, West Yorkshire, dating to the late eighteenth century. The chairs include an array of symbols that represent the Officers of the lodge; the Sun for the Worshipful Master, the plumb for the Junior Warden and the level for the Senior Warden. The lodge took its name from the Senior Warden's chair which says 'Amity and Probity'.

Why is the colour blue used on the aprons and collars?

Within Freemasonry, the colour blue is a symbol of universal friendship and benevolence. When sitting in the lodge room, the most common types of blue coloured regalia under the UGLE are the light blue for those below provincial rank or holding an Office, the darker garter blue with a gold striping for provincial rank, and the dark garter blue of Grand Lodge.

However, there are actually different colours used for some Officers, for example, Grand Stewards wear crimson colored regalia. Past Provincial Grand Stewards have the same but with a silver cord in the centre. Provincial Grand Stewards again wear the same, but slight variations include that the collar is only

and half inches broad as opposed the Grand Stewards which are four inches.

In the three remaining of the original four lodges which founded the Grand Lodge of England in 1717, the Officers are allowed to wear a stripe of 'garter blue' in the centre of the light blue collar. In the Prince of Wales Lodge No. 259, the Officers are allowed an edging of garter blue on their aprons. There is also the London Rank which is lined with garter blue, the aprons having the word 'London' on them.[96]

On a historical note, aprons were commonly hand made in the eighteenth and early nineteenth centuries, and many of these fine creative and personalised examples can be found on display in various Masonic Halls.

A silk Craft apron, which dates from the later nineteenth century. *Warrington Masonic Museum.*

The Grand Lodge apron of Sir Gilbert Greenall, first Baronet of Daresbury. The apron seems to be of a lighter colour to the usual Grand Lodge aprons, and has been dated to around the mid-nineteenth century. *Warrington Masonic Museum.*

What is the importance of the Working Tools?

The working tools of stonemasonry are presented to the candidate towards the end of each degree, and in Freemasonry, they represent the moralistic qualities of a Mason, and are part of the teachings a candidate acquires during his progressive journey. Here are the tools presented to the Entered Apprentice and Fellowcraft, along with a brief description of the symbolic meaning.

The 24-Inch Gauge

As a working tool of an Entered Freemason, the 24-Inch Gauge represents the 24 hours of the day; part to be spent in work, part in prayer, and

part in service of a friend or Brother in time of need. In this sense the 24-Inch Gauge works as a guide for the Mason's working day, and allows for the measurement of moralistic and spiritual practices throughout the day.

The Common Gavel

This is a working tool, which is used to '*knock off all superfluous knobs and excrescences*' and to smooth the stone—a tool which reminds us of the rough and smooth ashlars, but in a moralistic sense, it represents the force of conscience which suppresses vain and unbecoming thoughts that may interrupt the working day, so we can ultimately achieve purity and virtue.[97]

The Chisel

The working tools of an Entered Apprentice Freemason include the chisel, which is used by the stonemason to smooth and prepare the stone, rendering it fit for more expert workmen, but within 'Speculative' Freemasonry, it points out the advantages of education, from which we can gain knowledge to refine our understanding of the world.[98]

The Square

Another important example is the square, which is a working tool of a Fellowcraft Freemason (and of course, a central symbol within Freemasonry), which is used by the stonemason to adjust rectangular corners of buildings, bringing rude matter into due form. In Speculative Freemasonry however, the square, like other tools, teaches the Mason morality, and how to attain goodness and perfection.[99] In all, the working tools are tools of perfection, and they teach us as Masons how to be perfect in a moralistic way.

The Level

The Level proves horizontals, but it reminds us of equality, especially amongst Brethren, and that death— the grand leveler of all human greatness, will reduce us all to the same state, no matter who we are in life.[100] This suggests that Freemasonry was a society that promoted equality.

The Plumb Rule

This last working tool presented to the Fellowcraft, is likened to Jacob's ladder, and teaches us justness, to stay on the path of virtue and to be upright in nature throughout our life.[101] In essence, all of these working tools are used to represent how we should act in life; teaching us not only to be good Masons, but to be good people. Entwined with these moralistic themes, the tools also represent the educational journey of the Mason, and can remind us how to achieve perfection. These tools can also be seen to work with other symbols and objects in the lodge, such as the rough and smooth ashlars, which again represent the progressive journey of the Mason as he works towards perfection.

Have there always been festive boards after the lodge meetings?

There have always been festivities attached to lodge meetings, some lodges actually have their meal before the lodge meeting rather than after, and some lodges style themselves as Dining Lodges; lodges that specialise in a more distinguished dining experience. Feasting has always been a central part of Freemasonry, with a Grand Feast being held from the early eighteenth century on the day of St John the Baptist on the 24th of June.

English Masonic tradition has the first Grand Feast being held at the Goose and Gridiron Alehouse in St. Paul's Churchyard in London, in 1717. The Grand Feast became a central tradition for the Modern Grand Lodge, though the location changed throughout time, meeting in 1797 for example at Canonbury Tower, near Islington, London. A Grand procession to the Grand Feast also took place, though this was discontinued in 1745, and the various Provincial Grand Lodges also held a banquet during their meetings.

Before the union of 1813, local lodges, both 'Antient' and 'Modern', celebrated St John's Day in June with a feast, and another important feast being held on the 27th of December, which was the day of St John the Evangelist (the two dates reflecting not only a celebration of Christian feast days, but also the Summer solstice and Winter solstice). In fact, the Grand Lodge of Wigan, which continued the 'Antient' traditions, endeavoured to celebrate both the St. John's days as important feast dates until they re-joined the UGLE in 1913, electing their Grand Lodge Officers on St John the Evangelist Day.

Surviving lodge minutes from the eighteenth century recite how much alcohol was consumed before and after lodge meetings, displaying not only rather large alcohol bills, but reprimands for intoxicated lodge members. The large alcohol bills, along with bills for tobacco, were commonplace, with many lodges having to pay them off at a later date, drinking and smoking obviously being a vital part of the lodge night. From the many toast lists and Masonic songs that survive from the eighteenth and nineteenth centuries, drinking and dining was an essential part of the Masonic experience, and for the lodges that used a table in the actual lodge room, there would have been an eclectic mix of ritual and feasting.[102] Dining and feasting was thus entwined with the essence of Masonic brotherhood, creating a deeper bond between the brethren of the lodge.

A print revealing a 'Table Lodge' dated from 1766. *Warrington Masonic Museum.*

The 'Table Lodge' room of the Lodge of Sincerity, of the Wigan Grand Lodge, painted by James Miller, the last surviving member of the Wigan Grand Lodge. Table Lodges still occur in the USA. *Many thanks to Jim Miller for the image of the painting.*

Why is there clapping/ applause sometimes during the ritual and the festive board?

Sometimes in response to toasts or speeches by guests during the festive board the Director of Ceremonies may ask for the particular number of the lodge to be clapped by the brethren; say for example the number of the lodge is 4647, then there would be four claps, six claps, four claps then finally seven claps, all done quickly, catching a few brethren out along the way. On other occasions the Master or Director of Ceremonies may call on the brethren to clap three times or in some lodges, three times three.

Applause in the lodge room or the festive board may occur when the ritual has been done to a high standard, showing appreciation to a certain Brother; a perfect explanation of the tracing board for example or an explanation of the working tools.

Why are there so many toasts at the festive board?

Toasting the Monarch, the Grand Master, the Provincial Grand Master, and the respective Officers, is something that goes on in most lodges under the UGLE. The Master, Senior and Junior Warden are required to do a number of toasts, these vary in different lodges, and the Tyler's Toast is also a regular toast which closes the evening. Other toasts include the 9 o'clock toast—a toast for poor and distressed Freemasons around the world—and the toasting of visiting brethren.

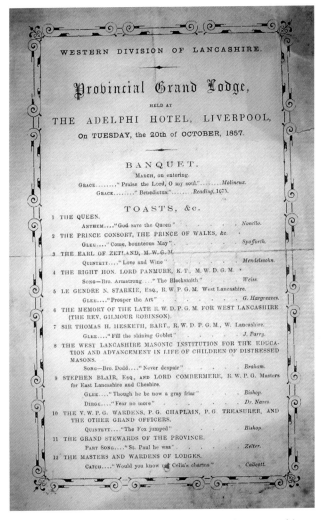

WESTERN DIVISION OF LANCASHIRE.

Provincial Grand Lodge,

HELD AT

THE ADELPHI HOTEL, LIVERPOOL,

On TUESDAY, the 20th of OCTOBER, 1857.

BANQUET.

MARCH, on entering.

GRACE........"Praise the Lord, O my soul."........*Molineux.*

GRACE........"Benedictus"........*Reading,* 1073.

TOASTS, &c.

1 THE QUEEN.
    ANTHEM...."God save the Queen" . . . . *Novello.*

2 THE PRINCE CONSORT, THE PRINCE OF WALES, &c.
    GLEE...."Come, bounteous May". . . . *Spofforth.*

3 THE EARL OF ZETLAND, M.W.G.M.
    QUINTETT...."Love and Wine" . . . . *Mendelssohn.*

4 THE RIGHT HON. LORD PANMURE, K.T., M.W.D.G.M.
    SONG—Bro. Armstrong...."The Blacksmith" . . *Weiss.*

5 LE GENDRE N. STARKIE, ESQ., R.W.P.G.M. West Lancashire.
    GLEE...."Prosper the Art" . . . . *G. Hargreaves.*

6 THE MEMORY OF THE LATE R.W.D.P.G.M. FOR WEST LANCASHIRE
    (THE REV. GILMOUR ROBINSON).

7 SIR THOMAS H. HESKETH, BART., R.W.D.P.G.M., W. Lancashire.
    GLEE...."Fill the shining Goblet" . . . . *J. Parry.*

8 THE WEST LANCASHIRE MASONIC INSTITUTION FOR THE EDUCA-
    TION AND ADVANCEMENT IN LIFE OF CHILDREN OF DISTRESSED
    MASONS.
    SONG—Bro. Dodd...."Never despair" . . . *Braham.*

9 STEPHEN BLAIR, ESQ., AND LORD COMBERMERE, R.W.P.G. Masters
    for East Lancashire and Cheshire.
    GLEE...."Though he be now a gray friar" . . *Bishop.*
    DIRGE...."Fear no more" . . . . *Dr. Nares.*

10 THE V.W.P.G. WARDENS, P.G. CHAPLAIN, P.G. TREASURER, AND
    THE OTHER GRAND OFFICERS.
    QUINTETT..."The Fox jumped" . . . . *Bishop.*

11 THE GRAND STEWARDS OF THE PROVINCE.
    PART SONG...."St. Paul he was". . . . *Zelter.*

12 THE MASTERS AND WARDENS OF LODGES.
    CATCH...."Would you know my Celia's charms" . *Callcott.*

A Toast list dating from 1857, from a Provincial Grand Lodge meeting of the Western Division of Lancashire at the Adelphi Hotel in Liverpool. Toasting has always been an important part of Masonic festivities, and can be traced to the early eighteenth century. *Warrington Masonic Museum.*

Do all lodges have Ladies' Nights and when does it date from?

Most lodges do have Ladies' Nights – an annual event in which the lodge celebrates the support the wives and girlfriends have given the members of the lodge over the year; an event not to be missed, if only to catch the exquisite vocal talents of a lodge member performing his rendition of the 'Ladies' Song'! Most Masons will never forgot the glitz of the sparkly ball gowns, evening attire, and the five course meals of a Ladies' Night, and the fact that there is always enough wine consumed to keep a new world vineyard in business for years to come!

The evening, besides being a special event for the Master and his wife or partner, is also an opportunity to introduce prospective candidates to Freemasonry, and to support the lodge charities. Historically, the exact date of the Ladies' Night is unknown, but Masonic Balls and festivities, in which Masons and non-Masons attended with their wives or partners, can be traced back to the eighteenth century. By the nineteenth century, many newspapers and Masonic magazines reported on these Balls, and though not classed specifically as 'Ladies' Nights', it would seem from the speeches, that these events produced an opportunity to thank the Ladies for their support.[103] Some Masonic Balls, such as the one held in Liverpool in 1864, was in aid of the funds of the West Lancashire Masonic Educational Institution, and was attended by numerous Masonic and local dignitaries.[104] This Grand Masonic Ball was widely reported in the local press, and had Stewards, which assisted in receiving the prestigious guests, some of the gentlemen actually wearing their Masonic regalia. The Ball had a lavish orchestra, and was richly decorated with a banner of the Grand Lodge, the supper room being decorated with banners of the Chapter.[105]

Ladies' Nights became increasingly fashionable after the Great War, and it was common for them to be reported in the local newspapers, such as on the 25th of February 1925, when the Riverside Lodge No. 4201 held a 'Ladies' Night' at the Masonic Hall, Clifton Road, Birkenhead. On the evening, a 'Whist Drive' and 'Dinner Dance' took place. A week later an article appeared in the Local Press, describing the evening and giving a detailed description of each of the Ladies' gowns.[106]

A Ladies Night menu for Domville Lodge No. 4647, dating from 1962. *Warrington Masonic Museum.*

What is Masonic Fire?

The earliest known reference to such a practice in England is contained in the exposé *Three Distinct Knocks*, published in 1760, in which it mentions that:
'*Every Man has a Glass set him, and a large Bowl of Punch, or what they like, is set in the Centre of the Table; and the senior Deacon charges (as they call it) in the North and East, and the junior Deacon in the South and West; for it is their duty to do so, i.e., to fill all the Glasses.*

Then the Master takes up his Glass, and gives a Toast to the King and the Craft, with Three Times Three in the Prentice's; and they all say Ditto, and drink all together, minding the Master's Motion: They do the same with the empty Glass that he doth; that is, he draws it a-cross his Throat Three Times..., and then makes Three Offers to put it down; At the third, they all set their Glasses down together, which they call firing: Then they hold the Left-hand Breast-high, and clap Nine Times with the Right, their Foot going at the same Time: When this is done, they all sit down.'[107]

'Firing' may have originated from the military, and Masonic 'fire' with Brethren crashing down thick-based drinking glasses on the table was once a common practice, but now it seems the clapping of hands is used as a substitute instead.

Firing toasts can be found in all Masonic Orders, such as the Rose Croix, which has a firing toast after speeches. With the right forefinger you cross yourself in the shape of the cross of St Andrew and point away from yourself (but not at anybody).[108]

Why do lodges use tracing boards?

Lodges use tracing boards to assist in telling the Masonic drama of the three Craft degrees. Lodges under the Grand Lodge of Ireland do not use tracing boards. The tracing boards that most UGLE lodges use are the Harris tracing boards, but in the eighteenth and early nineteenth centuries, lodges sometimes made their own either by painting canvas or boards. Evidence of these somewhat rustic examples can be seen within the Lodge of Sincerity in Wigan, Lancashire, when it was under the Grand Lodge of Wigan, and the third degree tracing board which was in the procession of the Lodge of Honour in Bath, which displayed pre-Union symbols such as a beehive, Noah's Ark and the hourglass.[109] Similarly, the York Grand Lodge had a tracing board which can still be seen at the Masonic Hall in York, which was locally painted, dating to 1778, and has older symbols such as the pyramid, oak leaves and mistletoe.[110]

The eighteenth century Masonic exposé *Three Distinct Knocks* displays a diagram which was drawn on the floor of the lodge in chalk and charcoal, as a guide for the degree ceremony.[111]

The Lodge of Lights in Warrington, old Lancashire, has two sets of tracing boards, both dating to the mid nineteenth century, and were both painted by local artists, though both are based on the traditional Harris designs. The accompanying pictures reveal a study of the symbols displayed on the tracing boards, painted with oils on a canvas, now slightly damaged through their use over the centuries, which have assisted in many Initiations, Passings and Raisings over the years.

A study of three tracing boards belonging to the Warrington Masonic Hall, oil on canvas, dated to the mid nineteenth century, and painted by a local artist.

Where does 'squaring the lodge' come from?

Squaring the lodge in a clockwise fashion (see the question on walking clockwise in the lodge) is obviously symbolic of the precision and perfection when working in the lodge, and is a reference to the actual symbol of the square. It may have also had its origins for more practical reasons; for during the eighteenth century the floor of the lodge room was drawn in chalk and charcoal, and it would be sensible to avoid the floor drawing so as not to smudge or erase it. The lodge of course, is also a representation of sacred ground, so to 'square the lodge', is to respect the ground as one would respect a Church or Mosque.

Is a special Bible used during the ceremony?

Some lodges do use tradition Bibles, such as the Geneva Bible dating from 1599, used by the Lodge of Lights in Warrington, reputed to be the same Bible that Elias Ashmole took his Masonic oath on.[112] The King James Bible, which President George H. W. Bush took his oath of office on in 1989, is from a lodge based in Manhattan called St John's Lodge. George Washington, who was a Freemason, was the first US President to take his oath of office on it in 1789, the Bible being supplied from the lodge, as there was no other Bible to hand. George W. Bush had hoped to take his oath of office on the same

Bible in 2001, but due to the heavy rain, a decision was made not to use it. Other lodges use tradition Bibles that have been in their lodges since their consecration, or ones that they have acquired from other lodges. Lodges also use the *Quran* and other holy books for the oath.

Another early Bible used in the Lodge of Edinburgh is the Breeches Bible, which was printed in 1587.

The 1599 Bible used by the Warrington based Lodge of Lights. According to lodge tradition, this was the Bible that Elias Ashmole took his oath on in 1646. *Warrington Masonic Museum.*

Did lodges really meet on the night of a full moon?

Yes, some lodges in the country and in towns met on the night of a full moon; though it is a far from sinister reason why they did this. During the eighteenth and early part of the nineteenth century when there was no street lighting, the more rural lodges met when there was a full moon so they could make the most of the light when they traveled to and from the lodge. Some older lodges still traditionally meet on, or as close to the night of a full moon as possible, such as the Lodge of Loyalty which meets in Prescot, Lancashire, and was founded in 1753, and the Royal Forest Lodge, founded in 1829, which meets in Waddington, also in Lancashire, both meeting on the Wednesday before the full moon.[113] In Vermont in the US, lodges that met within the week of the full moon during the nineteenth century were referred to as 'Moon Lodges'. The Moon is also an important symbol within Freemasonry and in the Webb ritual used in the US; the Moon is referred to as one of the three lesser or movable lights.[114]

Where does the term 'blackballing' come from?

The term 'blackballing' is perhaps as popular in the public mind when discussing Freemasonry as 'rolling the trouser leg up.' It creates a mysterious image, and for new members, to partake in a ballot for the first time, this sometimes comes to mind, and there has been many a joke in lodges during balloting about possible blackballing.

The use of balloting using black and white balls in lodges dates way back to the eighteenth century, the method being a democratic, though anonymous means of electing new candidates and joining members, and to settle disputes within the lodge—a secret ballot in effect. So if, when a candidate is proposed and balloted for, a brother feels that he is not the right person to be involved in Freemasonry, they can choose a black ball, whereas if they favour the candidate, they would choose a white ball.

For example, in the Lodge of Probity, a lodge founded in 1738 which still meets in Halifax, Yorkshire, it was recorded in the minutes on the 10th of August, 1763, that a certain Robert Kelly was rejected as a new member with a ballot of '*five yes, and seven no*'.[115] In the same lodge, after a dispute between two brethren, balloting was used to determine whether either or both brethren should be expelled, and in January 1767, a final ballot was taken to determine whether one of the brethren should be readmitted as a member, the result being recorded thus:

'For: 12 good masons
Against: 6 bad Brors.'

It was thus agreed that this particular brother could visit and the dispute should never be brought up in the lodge again.[116] In the York 'Union' Lodge, a lodge founded in 1777, the use of black and white balls for balloting was evident, as on 19th January, 1778, the lodge blackballed a new candidate and no reason was given. He obviously just wasn't the right type of person for the lodge![117]

Other societies that became increasingly popular in the nineteenth century, such as the Oddfellows, also used a similar system of balloting, and there was even an instance of a 'Discussion Class' held at the Mechanics' Institute in Warrington, Lancashire, using a similar method of balloting, proposing new members which had to be accepted by a majority; the class tried to become exclusive and twice rejected a would-be 'debater' on grounds of class, leading to the rules being changed.[118]

The use of black and white balls, also reflects the use of white and black within the lodge; the chequered floor of the lodge room and the use of dark clothing and white gloves, giving the working of the lodge an overall theme as well as a striking visual effect, reflecting the light and darkness of human nature; the black choice a negative one, the white choice being positive.

In rule 190 of the 1919 edition of the *UGLE Constitutions*, it states that '*No person can be made a Mason in, or*

admitted a member of, a Lodge, if, on ballot, three black balls appear against him; but the by-laws of a Lodge may enact that one or two black balls shall exclude a candidate'.[119] Thus, an effective and indeed, a flexible way of balloting has been used for centuries within lodges, to guarantee that '*no Lodge should introduce into Masonry a person whom the Brethren consider unfit to be a member of their own Lodge.*'[120] Today, some lodges use a 'yes' or 'nay' box instead of black and white balls for voting.

How were lodges lit prior to the introduction of electricity? What type of lighting was used and what was its arrangement in the lodge room?

Lighting in the lodge room was supplied by candles prior to the introduction of electricity; the effect creating a more subdued and mysterious atmosphere. An example of lodge lighting by the use of candles is shown in the eighteenth century Initiation print, the picture revealing a number of light sources including a candle chandelier, a lit candle by the Master to the right of the print, and a candle on the floor of the lodge to the left. There are also lodge cashbooks that indicate the purchase of candles and candlesticks, such as the Lodge of Probity in Halifax, which record the purchase of three candlesticks on the 24th of November 1762, at a cost of 14 shillings and sixpence.[121] They are still used by the lodge today.

The London based Lodge of Antiquity No. 2, one of the original four lodges that formed the 'Premier' Grand Lodge in 1717, also has a pair of mahogany candlesticks, which, according to the tradition of the lodge, once belonged to Sir Christopher Wren, the architect of St. Paul's Cathedral.[122]

Do lodges still participate in public processions?

Rule No. 178 in the *UGLE Book of Constitutions* states that '*No Brother shall appear clothed in any of the jewels, collars or badges of the Craft, in any procession, meeting or assemblage at which persons other than Masons are present, or in any place of public resort, unless the Grand Master or the Provincial or District Grand Master... shall have previously given a dispensation...*'[123] So, without the dispensation from either the Grand Master or Provincial Grand Master, no public processions or appearances in Masonic clothing can take place.

Masonic public processions have become quite rare, but this was not always the case; from 1723 the 'Premier/Modern' Grand Lodge took part in processions that consisted of an elegant carriage parade, with the Grand Master Elect being escorted by distinguished Masons dressed in full regalia through the London Streets. In the early 1740s, mock processions were organised by the opponents of the Grand Lodge, and the procession

to the Grand Feast was discontinued in 1745.[124] There is evidence that at local level, Masonic public processions continued, and certainly the 'York' Grand Lodge permitted processions, as can be seen with the Druidical Lodge at Rotherham; the Brethren taking part in a procession '*in proper clothing*' to the Parish Church from their meeting place in the Red Lion, on their day of Consecration on the 22nd of December, 1778.[125]

In the late Regency, Victorian and Edwardian periods, it was very common for lodges to be involved in local society and take part in very public processions wearing full Masonic regalia, be it for the coronation of a new monarch or the laying of a cornerstone or keystone for a new church, school, museum, library or Masonic Lodge.

There are countless examples of lodges taking part in a public display, such as the Lodge of Lights in Warrington, which marched through the town to celebrate the coronation of George IV on 19th July of 1821,[126] and on 22nd December 1836, the Lodge of Lights held a lavish ceremony for the laying of the keystone of a new bridge over the River Mersey, leaving a number of offerings, including a Masonic glass box, showing the set square and compass, and a number of coins. The son of the architect of the bridge, George Gamon of Knutsford, was specially made a Freemason just so he could participate in the ceremony. A procession had taken place from the

Market Hall to the bridge, and boys from the Bluecoat School also took part in the procession, along with local Constables and Churchwardens. Other lodges were involved in the procession such as the Lodge of Harmony from Liverpool.[127]

The Grand Lodge of Wigan also paraded through Wigan on 28th June 1838 to celebrate the coronation of Queen Victoria. As the nineteenth century progressed, Provincial Grand Lodges seemed to be more directly involved in the actual ceremonies, such as the Masonic ceremony described as taking place on 22nd August, 1843, when the Cheshire Provincial Grand Lodge fixed the keystone in the window of the New Church at Over, Cheshire. The mystical ceremony was concluded with '*coins of the present reign, together with descriptions of the day's proceedings, the names of the local authorities ext., deposited in a cavity in the stone.*'[128]

In the US, Masonic processions and ceremonies were also commonplace; perhaps the most celebrated and historical public ceremony took place on 18th September 1793, when President George Washington officiated at the laying of the cornerstone for the United States Capitol building. George Washington was dressed in Masonic regalia, and led a procession of officers and brethren from Maryland and Virginia to the site in the District of Columbia. Using a trowel, Washington deposited a silver plate and laid it on the cornerstone, and corn, wine, and oil

were placed on the stone after it was set in place. There was also a cornerstone ceremony for the University of Virginia, on the morning of 6th October 1817, which was laid with a Masonic ceremony with James Monroe applying the square and plumb. Thomas Jefferson and James Madison were also present, even though they were not Masons.[129]

Public processions wearing Masonic regalia still regularly occur in the US, a recent example occurring with the Grand Lodge of Indiana and the Prince Hall Grand Lodge of Indiana in August 2011, when over 100 Brethren from both Grand Lodges walked to the Statehouse to rededicate the statue of George Washington there. The event marked the 258th anniversary of George Washington's elevation to a Master Mason.[130]

However, in England during the recent Diamond Jubilee year of 2012, there were a number of Masonic marches, some wearing regalia, such as the Freemasons of Rugby, Warwickshire, who paraded through the town along with various local clubs and charities. Like the aforementioned procession in the US, the procession culminated with the unveiling of a commemorative plaque in honour of the occasions. Events like this are indeed rare in England today, but when done, they are very similar to how they were conducted back in the Victorian and Edwardian eras.[131] Masonic Church services still take place, and in some cases, Masonic regalia can be worn inside the Church during the service.

Did other Freemasons once use swords during the ceremony other than the Tyler?

There are many prints from the eighteenth century showing the Masonic ritual being conducted within a lodge room, with the Masons present using or wearing swords. This may be to add drama to the print, a touch of artistic license perhaps, or it could be because most men during the period would have actually carried swords for their own protection, particularly whilst traveling, in an age of highwaymen and duelling. These swords may have been called upon during the ceremony, especially to give a more dramatic effect whilst the initiate was giving his obligation. Indeed, a dagger, poignard, or the point of a compass, is of course, still used on the Candidate inside the lodge by the Inner Guard, and the Tyler still has his ceremonial sword. The Tyler's sword is always drawn to keep away Cowan's and intruders, and swords are also associated with the Knights Templar.

However, some lodges in certain jurisdictions still use swords within the ceremony; such as Lodge St Andrew No. 6, which is now under the United Grand Lodge of Queensland, but was previously under the Scottish Constitution. The lodge uses an arrangement of crossed swords across the bottom step of the Worshipful Master's pedestal, creating a diamond shape that the Senior Deacon has to step into when taking the minute book to have signed.[132]

The use of the sword within Freemasonry resounds in the title of Grand Sword Bearer, the Office symbolised by *two swords in saltire with a ribbon across the centre*. The Office of Inner Guard is also symbolised by the crossed swords, or *two swords in saltire*. Another enigmatic symbol is of the sword pointing to the naked heart, a symbol, which alludes to the sacred obligation that the initiate has to take. It has been said by the Masonic writer Kenneth Mackenzie, that the Tyler's sword was originally a 'wavy' sword,[133] which represented the flaming sword that had been placed in the East of the Garden of Eden, guarding its entrance, as mentioned in the *Book of Genesis*. There is a rare surviving example of the 'wavy' Tyler's sword placed in a stand, which is on display at a lodge in Beverley, Yorkshire, and a similar sword is in the possession of a lodge in Alnwick, Northumbria.[134]

Another historical Tyler's sword (though not a wavy sword) can be seen on display at the Swansea Masonic Temple in South Wales. It was seized from the hands of a French sailor at Fishguard in 1797, during the last attempted invasion of Britain by a French force, which landed in South Wales. According to the story, the invading French sailor was about to mercilessly cut down an innocent civilian, but before he could do so, he was himself slain, and on 1st June, 1805, the sword was presented to the Tyler of the Indefatigable Lodge No. 237, by a certain Brother Mathias.[135]

A Masonic sword revealing an array of stylised Masonic symbolism.
Photograph by Kathryn McCone Usher.

Do you have to go through the Master's Chair to get Provincial honours?

No. Long service in the lodge, and serving other offices such as Secretary could earn you Provincial honours. Dedication and work within the lodge, such as participating in charity events and being active in the social events of the lodge is also recognised. There are of course many different ranks at Provincial level and at Grand Lodge level; so one can be promoted at different times during one's Masonic career.

London Honours however are different; Metropolitan Grand Lodge has three awards only. They are:

1) London Rank—for non-Installed Masters, after at least ten years as a member and holding a non-progressive office for at least seven years.

2) London Grand Rank—awarded after a minimum of ten years as a member and no less than 5 years out of the Chair.

3) Senior London Grand Rank—awarded after a minimum of five years after London Grand Rank and remaining active both in their own lodge and within London Masonry.[136]

Masonic Symbolism

Where does all the symbolism come from?

Masonic symbols come from various sources; some like the square and compasses are obvious symbols that connect modern 'speculative' Freemasonry with the medieval stonemasons. Other symbols such as the sun and the moon, the pentagram, and the skull and cross bones seem more magical. The pentagram was commonly used by alchemists and magicians of the sixteenth and seventeenth centuries such as John Dee for example, and was used as a symbol of friendship by the early Scottish Freemason Sir Robert Moray.[137]

Freemasonry has used many symbols; symbols relating to the ritual and symbols representing the Officers. Those such as the beehive and the scythe are pre-Union symbols and are now redundant in many lodges, but other symbols, such as the sun and the moon, and the skull and crossed bones still survive and feature heavily in the Emulation Ritual in England. The sprig of acacia represents life, being placed on the grave of Hiram Abiff, and is an element of the Masonic drama. Other symbols represent the moralistic side of Freemasonry, such as the 24-inch gauge, the common gavel and the chisel.

The more enigmatic symbols of Freemasonry, such as the skull and crossbones, pomegranates, the sprig of acacia, the symbol of infinity, and the Ouroboros (the snake eating its own tail), are ancient symbols of life, death and rebirth, and relate to the Third Degree; the new Master Mason having being reborn into the enlightenment of Freemasonry, this dramatic part of the Masonic journey revealing the murder and burial of Hiram Abiff and the search for lost knowledge.[138]

The many symbols of office, such as Mercury, and the Dove and olive branch for the Deacons, the plumb for the Junior Warden, the level for the Senior Warden, and the 47th Problem of Euclid for the Past Master, not only signify the duties assigned to that particular office, but also have certain moralistic and educational overtones, some of which will be discussed within this book.[139]

The symbols of Freemasonry, taken from the 1769 edition of the *Constitutions*. *Warrington Masonic Museum*.

57

Third degree symbols taken from the 1769 edition of the *Constitutions. Warrington Masonic Museum.*

Why are there symbols that are used in Freemasonry which appear on tarot cards?

There are indeed symbols, which are included in many modern decks of tarot cards that are also used within Freemasonry, most notably with the suite of pentacles, the pentacle being a common symbol used in Masonry. Other notable tarot cards with obvious Masonic symbols are the High Priestess, who is pictured seated between two pillars, and in the Rider-Waite-Smith tarot deck, the two pillars are marked with a 'B' on the left and a

'J' on the right, referring to Boaz and Jachin, representing the two pillars at the entrance of Solomon's Temple. The High Priestess also displays pomegranates decorating the background, which also feature within the Third Degree of Freemasonry. Another tarot card with a symbol associated with Freemasonry is the Magician card; the symbol of infinity being situated above the head of the magician. Other symbols which can be found within Freemasonry that appear on the tarot cards include the crossed swords and the sun and the moon. This use of Masonic symbolism can be traced to the creative input of Freemason, Occultist and writer Arthur Edward Waite.

Waite co-created the influential Rider-Waite-Smith tarot card deck, which was published in 1909, and is still one of the most popular tarot card decks used today; the deck going on to influence other popular decks such as the Morgan-Greer Tarot. Waite took a keen and almost obsessive interest in the occult, becoming deeply involved with psychic research. He also became a member of the Hermetic Order of the Golden Dawn in 1891, and saw the symbolism of Freemasonry as having the same original source as other esoteric belief systems, such as alchemy, Kabbalism and Rosicrucianism; all providing a pathway to enlightenment through the search for hidden knowledge.[140]

Does the 'figure-of-eight' snake clasp on the aprons signify anything?

The snake in a 'figure-of-eight' position is similar to the symbol of infinity ∞, a never-ending flux without any limit, which reflects the theme of immortality within Freemasonry; the Master Mason rising from the figurative grave during the Third Degree. The symbol of infinity appears within Freemasonry as early as the eighteenth century, appearing for example in a print of various Masonic symbols in a copy of the 1769 *Book of Constitutions*.

The concept of the nature of infinity has its roots in ancient Greek and Indian philosophy, though the symbol itself is often accredited to the seventeenth century English mathematician John Wallis, who was part of a group of natural philosophers that evolved into the Royal Society. The symbol is used within mathematics denoting an unbounded limit.[141]

How old is the Ouroboros symbol?

Ouroborus

The Ouroboros symbol—the snake eating its own tail—can be traced to Ancient Egypt, and occurs in many other cultures, such as in Norse mythology, where it appears as Jörmungandr. The Ouroboros symbol was adopted by the Alchemists of the early modern period; its circular representation of eternal life and infinity being alluded to in esoteric works of the seventeenth century such as *The Garden of Cyrus* by Thomas Browne.[142] Like the infinity symbol, the Ouroboros symbol is featured in Freemasonry, finding a home next to other symbols of life, death and rebirth, and can be seen on the centenary jewel of the UGLE.[143]

What does the Beehive within Freemasonry signify and why did it become disused in England?

The beehive was a popular symbol within Freemasonry during the eighteenth century, but became disused in England after the union of the 'Moderns' and the 'Antients' in 1813. The beehive represents the working lodge, and there are usually seven bees to be seen flying around the beehive, representing the seven Masons needed to open the lodge. The beehive is an ancient symbol, being used in the Egyptian, Roman and Medieval periods, and was also quickly adopted by Friendly Societies and Co-Operative Societies, the symbol representing industry; that if people work together for the same goal then it can be achieved (which in essence, is what Freemasonry is about). One bee alone cannot survive, but with others working industrially in a hive, it thrives to produce life-giving honey. Some Co-operative societies even used bees in their names, an example being the Daisyfield Industrial Bees Co-operative Society. The beehive symbol was also used by the Provident Mutual Life Assurance, which was originally founded in 1840. Perhaps because it became commonly associated with Friendly Societies and Trade Unions, its popularity within English Freemasonry waned and it became redundant after the union, though the beehive remained popular in American Freemasonry.

A pre-union Masonic jug, dating from the late 1790s-1810, revealing symbols such as the All-Seeing Eye and on its reverse, the beehive. *Warrington Masonic Museum.*

What did the Ark symbolise within Freemasonry and why is it no longer used?

The Ark symbol within Freemasonry, like the beehive, became disused after the union in 1813, perhaps because of its obvious Biblical connection, although, along with the beehive, it was still used by the Grand Lodge of Wigan, which practiced the 'Antient' ritual, and both symbols appeared on a Tracing Board for the Lodge of Sincerity, the main lodge of the Wigan based Grand Lodge.[144] The Ark is usually combined with an anchor, and together they are symbols of well-spent life; the Ark being a symbol of faith, and the anchor a symbol of hope, hence the number of lodges that have 'faith' and 'hope' in their name. The moralistic and Biblical imagery of the Ark is striking, and also reminds us that the Ark was constructed with instructions from God, and like the beehive, the symbol remained popular in American Freemasonry.

When did the All-Seeing Eye become a Masonic Symbol?

The All-Seeing Eye, or Eye of Providence, can be traced back to Egypt, appearing as the Eye of Horus, and it only became a Masonic symbol at the turn of the eighteenth century, when, in 1797, it was used in Thomas Smith Webb's *Freemasons Monitor*, although there are a number of surviving hand crafted aprons which reveal the Eye of Providence dating to slightly earlier. The All-Seeing Eye is effectively the eye of God, watching a Mason at all times as he practices the moralistic principles of the Craft, and the symbolism featured prominently in French Revolutionary propaganda; the All-Seeing Eye being commonly used to portray the Enlightenment and justice brought about by the Revolution.[145] The All-Seeing Eye famously appears on the American one Dollar Bill, though this particular design only dates from 1935, a design which displays the reverse of the Great Seal of the United States, which was used from 1782. The All-Seeing Eye appears in English Freemasonry as part of the jewel of the Grand Master; set within a triangle and placed between the extended compasses.[146]

The Masonic window in St. John the Evangelist Church in Knotty Ash, Liverpool, showing the All-Seeing Eye and a number of other Masonic and Royal Arch references. The window was dedicated in 1938 by a local lodge.

An Antient's apron dating to c.1789. It reveals the All-Seeing Eye set in a triangle. Certain later eighteenth century aprons feature this symbolism. The apron is held at the library and museum of Tapton Hall.

The All-Seeing Eye displayed on a ceiling in Haigh Hall, Wigan in Lancashire. Haigh Hall belonged to the prominent local Freemason Lord Lindsay, who was a founder of the Wigan based Lindsay Lodge in 1870.

Why does the Past Master's Jewel display the 47th Problem of Euclid?

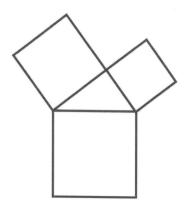

Past Master's Symbol

The 47th Problem of Euclid, first discovered by Pythagoras, displays the basis of all proportional geometry and represents perfect architecture, symbolising its divinity. It appeared on the frontispiece of the first edition of the *Constitutions* in 1723,[147] and it is vital to architecture as it creates a square, used to check angles of ninety degrees, which of course is a vital tool used in Freemasonry. The Egyptians used a simple method of creating a square; by taking a rod, which was three cubits long, another measuring four cubits long, and a third rod measuring five cubits long, when placed together as a tri-angle, the angle where the three and four cubit rods met was always a right angle.

The unit of measurement could be anything; a cubit, a foot, an inch, just as long as it was relative to the 3-4-5 measuring method. The use of this 3-4-5 method of measuring is symbolised in some lodges by taking the Entered Apprentice around the lodge three times in the First Degree, four times in the Second and five times in the Third Degree, so the Mater Mason finally completes his journey having been inducted symbolically into the sacred measuring technique. After serving as Master of the lodge, he becomes more complete and perfect, and having symbolically built a sacred and divine building, which is true and right, and symbolically managed his workforce, he is thus rewarded with the symbol (which contains the most powerful geometrical knowledge) on his jewel when he leaves the Office, so he can continue to guide the lodge in maintaining continued perfection.

A post-union Masonic dinner plate, revealing symbols which are still recognisable in all English lodges today. *Warrington Masonic Museum.*

Is the square also referred to as a set-square or T-square?

The square, which appears with the compass (or to be precise, a set of compasses joined together) to produce the most popular symbol of Freemasonry, has been referred to as a set-square and as a T-square by different writers over the centuries, though in the present ritual, it is simply referred to as a square. For example, in Edward Dobson's *A Rudimentary Treatise on Masonry and Stonecutting*, published in 1849, Dobson describes the '*set-square*' as one of '*the principal drawing instruments required by the mason*' along with the compass,[148] and the 'set-square' is again mentioned with the compass in the popular *Signs and Symbols Bible* as the '*the-best known symbol associated with Freemasonry*'.[149] Historian Edward Batley also refers to the term 'set-square' as being used as part of the '*mason's insignia*' during the eighteenth century.[150]

The modern definition of a set-square, square and a T-square in the Oxford dictionary is as follows:

- **Set-square**: A right-angled triangular plate for drawing lines, especially at 90°, 45°, 60°, or 30°.[151]
- **Square**: An L-shaped or T-shaped instrument for obtaining or testing right angles.[152]
- **T-square**: A T-shaped instrument for drawing or testing right angles.[153]

So, a square is perhaps the best way to describe the Mason's working tool, though the word set-square has been used to describe the same tool, and indeed, been used to describe the same symbol over the centuries by various writers.

Some Deeper Considerations

What other Masonic side Orders are there?

There are numerous, and rather colourful side Orders, all giving a different perspective on Freemasonry, and offering a new insight into the search for lost knowledge. There is the Royal Arch, Mark Masonry, Royal Ark Mariners (which is a separate degree conferred on Mark Master Masons), there are Christian Orders such as the Red Cross of Constantine and the Knights Templar, and more esoteric Orders such as the Rosicrucian Society of England. The many side Orders continue to explore similar moralistic themes within Freemasonry, and in the case of side Orders such as the Red Cross of Constantine and the Knights Templar, the Master Mason has to be a member of the Royal Arch. However, there are side Orders that a Master Mason can join without being a member of the Royal Arch in England and Wales, such as the Order of the Secret Monitor or the Order of Mark Master Masons.[154]

These side Orders have a somewhat parallel history to Craft Freemasonry; the Royal Arch for example, has obscure origins, possibly dating to the early 1740s, and was considered as a fourth Degree by the 'Antient' Grand Lodge, but on the union of 'Antient' and 'Modern' Grand Lodges in 1813, the Royal Arch in England and Wales came to be seen officially as the completion of the Third Degree. The Grand Lodge of Master Mark Masons was founded in 1856, but has earlier origins, its practice being traced to the late eighteenth century, which was similar to the Red Cross of Constantine, which, despite having the Grand Imperial Conclave reassembled in 1865, can also be traced back to the late eighteenth century. The Red Cross of Constantine, the Knights Templar and the Order of the Secret Monitor are all based at the Mark Masons Hall, St. James Street, London.

These side Orders offer the continuation of the Masonic journey, and give the Freemason a choice in exploring other pathways. In other jurisdictions, such as in the US, further degrees are offered in other forms, such as the Scottish Rite, which enables the Mason to complete up to 33 degrees.[155]

What is the Scottish Rite?

The desire to explore further degrees and study Masonic mysteries in the USA led to the success of the 'Ancient and Accepted Rite' commonly referred to the 'Scottish Rite', which was nurtured from an obscure Masonic practice in the early 1800s to a Rite of foremost importance by the attorney, Confederate officer and Freemason Albert Pike. The Scottish Rite enables the Mason to complete 33 Degrees, each ritual revealing deeper mysteries to the Freemason as he continues his journey to gain the ultimate 33rd Degree. The Scottish Rite is open for Master Masons from Craft or Blue Masonry, and in essence, opens up a progressive journey.

Albert Pike received the 4th to the 32nd Degree in South Carolina in 1853 from the Masonic writer Dr Albert G. Mackey, eventually receiving the 33rd degree and becoming the Grand Commander for the Southern Jurisdiction in the USA. The Scottish Rite has its beginnings in the later eighteenth century and like the 'Antients', it has been linked to Jacobite origins by certain writers. It was Pike however, who reworked and revised the rituals, and by 1872 he published the gargantuan work *Morals and Dogma of the Ancient and Accepted Scottish Rite of Freemasonry*. The Scottish Rite also captured the keen interest of Masonic writers Dr George Oliver and Dr Robert Thomas Crucefix in England, and together they helped to form the Supreme Council 33˚ in 1845, which was warranted by the Northern Jurisdiction in the USA.[156]

Pike's work cleverly promoted the Scottish Rite, and though quite a heavy read, it puts forward a tantalising glimpse of the innermost mysteries of this version of Freemasonry. It discusses Pike's theories on the degrees, giving 'lectures' on each, drawing knowledge from the Old Testament, the Kabbalah, and Pythagorean principles, and presents Pike's in-depth intellect on the secrets and symbolism of Freemasonry,

the search for the lost word of God, and the hidden mysteries of Nature and Science, which according to Pike *'was taught to Moses and Pythagoras'*.[157] The work became widely published and was accessible to all kinds of Freemasons, and despite being quite in-depth in discussing the lost word of God, he expertly guides the reader through the lectures of 32 degrees (the 33rd being the ultimate degree and is only revealed at the end of the physical Masonic journey).

One particular degree, the 13th, is called *The Royal Arch of Solomon* within the Southern Jurisdiction, and Pike puts forward how *'every Masonic Lodge is a temple of religion'*. He discussed how the Holy of Holies is a cube *'by which the ancients presented Nature'*; describing the Temple as having a *'starred'* ceiling and that *'every Masonic Lodge represents the Universe'*.[158] In its presentation of the Temple and the themes of the search for hidden knowledge—the lost word of God—this particular degree bears a slight resemblance to the Royal Arch ritual of the United Grand Lodge of England. The 18th Degree is called the Rose Croix, its name echoing a romantic connection to the Rosicrucians, the degree becoming of particular interest to Oliver and Crucefix, with Oliver discussing how the Rose Croix was believed to have been practiced by King Arthur and his Knights of the Round Table.[159] The Scottish Rite is proof of how Masons desired a deeper knowledge and a

A Quick Guide To Freemasonry

deeper understanding of Freemasonry, and how an organised progression to further degrees became popular. The Scottish Rite is currently practised all over the world.

What is the York Rite?

The York Rite is also an American Masonic organisation, but unlike the Scottish Rite, it is an assemblage of Masonic 'grades' or side Orders, including the Royal Arch, giving the Mason access to a progression of higher degrees such as the Mark Master degree and the Chivalric Orders of the Knights Templar. The name was inspired by the legend of Edwin who organised the first Grand Lodge of Masons in York in 926 AD, but is not linked historically to the independent Grand Lodge that operated in York, England, during the eighteenth century.[160] The Ancient York Rite was discussed in detail in *Duncan's Masonic Ritual and Monitor*, which was published in the USA in 1866, Duncan stating the purpose of the work being so the Mason could *'progress from grade to grade'*.[161]

Was the Royal Arch once a Fourth Degree?

The Royal Arch was once considered a Fourth Degree, especially by the 'Antient' Grand Lodge, which existed from 1751 to 1813, and was certainly practiced as a separate degree by the Wigan Grand Lodge, which existed from 1823 to 1913. The York Grand Lodge, which operated during the eighteenth century, also practiced the Royal Arch as a fourth

degree. It is now seen officially as the completion of the Third Degree under the UGLE, though the ritual takes place in a separate Chapter room and it takes the story forward to around 520 BC, when Jerusalem and Solomon's Temple were in ruins. In an effort to rebuild the Temple, the ruins are symbolically excavated to prepare the ground for the foundation of the second Temple, and in doing so the lost word of a Master Mason is re-discovered. The Royal Arch continues the theme of the search for knowledge, and possible remnants of the ceremony as a fourth degree can still be seen, such as when four knocks are heard at the door of the Chapter room, and when the First Principal rises from his chair four times, instead of the three times, which he does in Craft Freemasonry. The Chapter, or Convocations, as the meetings are referred to, meets three or four times a year, so the costs are relatively less than the Craft fees.

The Candidate enters the Chapter room blindfolded as a Master Mason, wearing his Master Mason apron, and, as the ceremony unfolds, the story is revealed in three parts; the first part consists of the Candidate being guided around the Chapter room by the Principal Sojourner (a journeyman mason) arriving at the vaulted chamber in the ruined Temple. An obligation is taken and the Master Mason is restored to light. In the second part, the Candidate is re-admitted after retiring from the Chapter room, and becomes

66

one of three Sojourners, members of the tribe of Judah, who offer their assistance in the rebuilding of the Temple, and are given the task of preparing the foundation, discovering a hidden vault. In the third part, the Sojourners give an explanation as to how the secret vault was re-discovered and the recovery of its long lost contents—the sacred lost word of a Master Mason. The candidate is rewarded and decorated as a Royal Arch Companion and is invested in a new set of regalia; the apron, which is still made of lambskin, is more colourful with a scarlet and purple border, a sash of the same colours and a jewel which can also be worn in the Craft lodge, symbolic of the links between Craft Masonry and the Royal Arch.

Is Freemasonry really about the Art of Memory?

The ancient discipline of the technique of memorisation is certainly a significant feature of Freemasonry, especially where the ritual is concerned. To remember the large parts of the ritual such as the Charge delivered by the Worshipful Master after the initiation ceremony is immensely impressive to say the least (five pages in the official Emulation Ritual book). The Art of Memory was used by the ancient Greeks and the Romans, and interest in it was revived during the Renaissance. The definition of the Art of Memory by the eminent Roman Philosopher Marcus Tullius Cicero (106-43 BC) is perhaps still the best example:

'persons desiring to train this faculty must select places and form mental images of the things they wish to remember and store those images in the places, so that the order of the places will preserve the order of the things, and the images of the things will denote the things themselves…'

In this sense, the mind is an ordered, sacred and calm place, where images are stored in order to represent what the person wishes to remember. If you look around the lodge room—a calm, sacred place—it is full of symbols, which represent certain elements that could help the Freemason remember, the Tracing Board is full of images which can assist in recall, and of course, the ritual itself has certain poetical elements, such as incidents of alliteration (*part or parts, point or points*), imagery (*to mark the setting sun*), the 'use of three' (*Brotherly love, relief and truth*), and on occasions, rhyming schemes (*conceal, and never reveal*) to assist the Freemason in remembering what he or she has to say.[162]

Is the lodge really a depiction of Solomon's Temple?

Yes, the lodge is symbolically a recreation of Solomon's Temple, best exemplified with the pillars of Jachin and Boaz, the symbolism on display such as the pomegranates, and, of course, the lodge being the setting for the theatre of the three degrees, the third of which is dramatically set within the Temple itself. The lodge constantly alludes to the Temple, which was the house of God, the dimensions of which were actually given by God. The search for the dimensions of Solomon's Temple, as written in the Old Testament of the Bible (the Book of Chronicles and also in the Book of Kings), were of keen interest to natural philosophers of the seventeenth century, such as Sir Christopher Wren and Sir Isaac Newton, who both recreated diagrams of what they believed the Temple to be like. This fascination can be seen in Renaissance architects such as Andrea Palladio and Juan Bautista Villalpando, and the celebration of the Temple in architecture can be plainly observed in Palladian structures such as Chiswick House in London.[163]

Dr Jean Theophilus Desaguliers, who I mentioned in an earlier answer as being responsible for the Third Degree ritual in the 1720s, was close to Sir Isaac Newton, and would have been aware of his research into understanding the sacred Biblical codes, especially Newton's work on understanding the Temple. As a celebration of architecture, initially given to man by God, it is easy to see how the third degree emerged from these fashionable ideas and concepts of the period.[164]

Wren's concept of St Paul's Cathedral in London was the embodiment of the Temple and also a celebration of the New Science, and it was the location of scientific experiments by Desaguliers. In the nineteenth century, Freemasons such as Sir Charles Warren, more famous now for his role as Commissioner of the Police during the Jack the Ripper case, actually excavated underneath Temple Mount and surveyed Herod's Temple in 1867, publishing his findings in a paper for the Transactions of the Quatuor Coronati Lodge.[165] Supposed stones from Solomon's Temple were also placed in St. Paul's Cathedral by archeologist James Fergusson, and the high alter of the Washington National Cathedral was made from stone quarried from Solomon's Quarry—which supposedly supplied the stone for Solomon's Temple.[166]

Thus, Solomon's Temple is a vital and central part of Freemasonry, and is celebrated in Craft Freemasonry. Royal Arch Freemasonry also celebrates the rebuilding of the Temple, but that is another story.

Is the apron really more ancient than the Golden Fleece or Roman Eagle?

The Golden Fleece appears in the ancient Greek mythology. The Order of the Golden Fleece was founded by Duke Phillip of Burgundy in 1430. The Roman Eagle was the symbol of the power and military might of the Roman Empire. The Order of the

Garter (which is also mentioned by the Senior Warden during the first degree ceremony) was created by King Edward III of England in 1348. The use of the apron as a badge could well be older than any of these, as stonemasons were certainly working on buildings and temples from ancient Greece and Rome.

Who was Hiram Abiff?

Hiram Abiff is mentioned during the Third Degree ritual as the principal architect of Solomon's Temple. It is '*Hiram, king of Tyre*' who is mentioned in the Bible, in chapter 5 of the first *Book of Kings*, who is said to have contributed to the building of the Temple, after Solomon commanded that great stones be used for the foundations: '*And Solomon's builders and Hiram's builders did hew them*'.[167] In the second *Book of Chronicles*, it states that '*King Huram of Tyre*' sent '*master Huram*' who was the son of a Danite woman and a Tyrian father, who, in a letter to Solomon, was described as '*an experienced worker in gold and silver, copper and iron, stone and wood, as well as in purple, violet, and crimson yarn, and in fine linen; he is also a trained engraver who will be able to work with your own skilled craftsmen and those of my lord David...*'[168]

The descriptions of Hiram king of Tyre and master Huram, can cause confusion, as '*master Huram*' is clearly referred to as the builder in the *Book*

of Chronicles, but Hiram king of Tyre, or Huram king of Tyre is mentioned in both the *Book of Kings* and the *Book of Chronicles*, and the former refers only to him as supplying '*timber, both cedar and pine*'—building materials from Lebanon, for Solomon's Temple.[169] In the eighteenth century exposé *Jachin and Boaz*, both Hiram king of Tyre and Hiram Abiff are clearly named as separate '*Grand Masters concerned in the building of Solomon's Temple*'.[170] The Bible however does not mention the death of Hiram and the Hiram story seems to have developed at a later date, perhaps in a medieval mystery tradition linked to the guilds.

The Masonic tradition of Hiram Abiff as the principle architect of the Temple who sacrificed himself for the secrets of the Craft, is a moralistic tale filled with symbolism and drama, and also echoes the eighteenth century interests in the search for lost knowledge and necromancy (the raising of the dead). After finding the grave of the murdered Hiram Abiff, he was 'raised' on the third attempt, and was reburied '*as near to the Sanctum Sanctorum as the Israelitish law would permit...*' As some of these questions and answers cross over into to each other, it is interesting that it stated towards the end of the third degree Hiram story that '*Fifteen trusty fellowcrafts attended the funeral, clothed in white aprons and gloves as emblems of their innocence*'.[171]

An actual skull and femur bones once used in the Third Degree raising ceremony.
It is unknown if they once belonged to a Freemason! *Warrington Masonic Museum.*

What are Noachidae?

Noachidae are described in Mackenzie's *Royal Masonic Cyclopaedia* as descendants of Noah, Noah being mentioned as the founder and father of Masonic theology. In James Anderson's second edition of the *Constitutions*, published in 1738, he puts forward that a Mason is to observe the moral law as a true Noachida,[172] and the Noah story, as told in the Old Testament, influenced various medieval mystery plays, such as the York Mystery Cycle, where the shipwrights performed 'The Building of the Ark' and the fishers and mariners performed 'The Flood'. Sir Christopher Wren also mentions that Noah's Ark was the first example of naval architecture, and there was a story, recorded on a manuscript dated 1726, which recites an attempt to raise Noah to gain secret knowledge, similar in essence to the attempt to raise Hiram Abiff during the Third Degree, leading to suggestions that the character of Noah could have been changed to Hiram during the creation of the this degree.[173]

Why were there a lot of poets and writers attracted to Freemasonry?

There have been a glittering array of renowned writers and poets involved in Freemasonry over the centuries; poets such as Robbie Burns, Alexander Pope and Branwell Brontë, and writers such as Jonathan Swift, Mark Twain, Rudyard Kipling, Sir Arthur Conan Doyle and Henry Rider Haggard, are just a small selection of the more famous, but other lesser known poets include Dr Jean Theophilus Desaguliers, the man behind the modernisation of the ritual, which has poetical elements. Indeed, it may be these poetical elements and the emotive drama of the Masonic ritual that initially attracted some of the writers, the ritual certainly inspiring some of their work, with Robbie Burns, Conan Doyle, Kipling and Rider Haggard all being influenced by Freemasonry, littering their work with Masonic references.

Members of the Authors' Club, an established gentleman's club based in London, actually founded the Authors' Lodge in 1910, a lodge in which Kipling was an honorary member, and the Quatuor Coronati Lodge, again based in London, was founded in 1884 as a research lodge, writers of Masonic history such as Sir Walter Besant, Sir Charles Warren and R.F. Gould being able to present their work and get papers published in the lodge's *Transactions.*[174]

Why were there so many Occultists linked to Freemasonry?

There were indeed a number of what was termed Occultists linked to Freemasonry, especially in the Victorian and Edwardian era, such as Sir Arthur Conan Doyle, Arthur Edward Waite, John Yarker and even the 'wickedest man in the world'— Aleister Crowley. In the Oxford dictionary, the meaning of the word 'occult' is given as being something that is 'beyond the range of ordinary knowledge',[175] thus the Occultists were searching for hidden knowledge, and in doing so, were sampling the delights of the forbidden fruit of their labours, be it in the exploration of spiritualism, tarot divination, or ritualistic and magical activities.

The exploration of Freemasonry, its history and its further degrees, or side Orders, were of particular interest to Arthur Edward Waite, who along with John Yarker, also ventured into Rosicrucianism.[176] Waite was also involved in the Hermetic Order of the Golden Dawn, an Order, which can be traced back to 1887, when leading esoteric Freemasons Dr William Wynn Westcott, the Rev. A.F.A. Woodford, and Samuel Liddell MacGregor Mathers assisted in founding the Order, which practised ceremonial magic, adopting various Masonic features. These Occult Freemasons were certainly attracted to the esoteric nature of the Craft, and were keen to research the hidden mysteries of nature and science; the search for mysterious lost knowledge, which resounded in the Masonic ritual appealing to their nature.[177]

What are the Three Lesser Lights of Freemasonry?

The three lesser lights are told to the candidate during the First Degree ceremony; they are the Sun (in the south) represented by the Junior Warden, the Moon (in the west) represented by the Senior Warden, and the Worshipful Master in the east.[178] These symbols are sometimes represented on the Officers chairs in older lodges, with the rising Sun sometimes being displayed on the Worshipful Masters chair.[179] These are reminiscent of the more ancient traditions of the worship of the Sun and the Moon, and the use of 'three' yet again within Freemasonry. In some jurisdictions, these lesser lights are represented by three candles, which are arranged in the position of a triangle on the altar; each being lit as soon as the lodge is opened.

Has the Masonic 'Sign of Distress' ever been used?

According to various traditions, yes it has been used, an example occurring during the American War of Independence, when Native American Joseph Brant, a Freemason and Mohawk Chief fighting for the British, recognised the Masonic sign of distress which was given by fellow Freemasons on the American side. Freemasonry was sometimes used to attract and secure the loyalty of certain members of the indigenous elite, bringing them closer to the British cause, such as in the case of Joseph Brant. Brant became a favourite of Sir William Johnson, the British Superintendent for Northern Indian

Affairs, who became close to the Mohawk people, and enlisted their allegiance in the French and Indian War. The young Brant took up arms for the British, and, after the war, Brant found himself working as an interpreter for Johnson.

Around 1775, after being appointed secretary to Sir William's successor, Guy Johnson, Brant received a Captain's commission in the British Army and set off for England, where he became a Freemason and confirmed his attachment to the British Crown; Brant's Masonic apron, according to legend, being presented to him by George III himself. On his return to America, Brant became a key figure in securing the loyalty of other Iroquois tribes in fighting for the British against the 'rebels' during the American War of Independence.

It was during the war that Brant entered into Masonic legend; after the surrender of the 'rebel' forces at the Battle of the Cedars on the St Lawrence River in 1776, Brant famously saved the life of Captain John McKinstry, a member of Hudson Lodge No.13 of New York, who was about to be burned at the stake. McKinstry, remembering that Brant was a Freemason, gave him the Masonic sign of appeal, which Brant instantly recognised, an action which secured McKinstry's release and subsequent good treatment. McKinstry and Brant remained friends for life, and in 1805, he and Brant visited the Masonic Lodge in Hudson, New York, where Brant was given an excellent reception. Brant's portrait now hangs in the lodge.

Another story relating to Brant during the war has another 'rebel' captive named Lieutenant Boyd giving Brant a Masonic sign, which secured him a reprieve from execution. However, on this occasion, Brant left his Masonic captive in the care of the British, who subsequently had Boyd tortured and executed. After the war Brant removed himself with his tribe to Canada, establishing the Grand River Reservation for the Mohawk people.[180]

Perhaps one of the most moving examples of Masonic brotherhood during the Civil War was written by American Masonic historian Joseph Fort Newton, who related the story of how his father, a Freemason and soldier in the Union army, had been taken prisoner, and while at a prisoner of war camp, had become seriously ill. He made himself known as a Mason to a Confederate officer in the camp, and the officer subsequently took him to his home and nursed him back to health. At the end of the war, the same Confederate officer gave Joseph Fort Newton's father money and a pistol for his journey home.[181]

Another incident that revealed how Freemasonry bridged the bitter political divide created by the Civil War was during the battle of Gettysburg in 1863, when the Confederate officer and Freemason Lewis Addison Armistead, who was mortally wounded in the field of battle, gave the Masonic sign for distress. Fellow Freemason Henry H. Bingham, who recognised the sign, attended to him, even though he was a Union officer. Armistead gave Bingham his personal effects to pass onto his old friend and fellow Mason Winfield Scott Hancock, who was also a Union officer.[182]

Freemasonry around the World

How many different types of lodges are there Worldwide?

There are many different types of lodges worldwide that practice different variations of Freemasonry; in the USA, they have State Grand Lodges, and as we shall see, in some States they hold lodge meetings outside! There are independent lodges, such as the Halcyon Lodge in Ohio;[183] there is Prince Hall Freemasonry, and the Scottish Rite, which provides an organised progression for Master Masons to explore up to 33 degrees. There are also Masonic organisations for women (The Order of the Eastern Star being one) and for young people (The Order of DeMolay and The International Order of the Rainbow for Girls—see below). Freemasonry is practiced in many countries all over the world; Africa, India, Asia, Mexico, South America, all over Europe, and it truly becomes a diverse and adaptable practice.

How does Freemasonry differ in the USA?

After the American War of Independence, the lodges in the newly formed United States had to choose how to organise themselves; most lodges were either under the 'Moderns' or the 'Antients'—both Grand Lodges operating from England, as well as the Grand Lodge of Scotland. They chose to organise themselves through Grand Lodges within the State; for example the Grand Lodge of Massachusetts traces its beginnings to 1733 and the Grand Lodge of the State of New York which was established in 1787 (though organised earlier in 1782) and the Grand Lodge of Pennsylvania which was established in 1786. It wasn't long before variations of ritual practice developed, such as the Ritual of Pennsylvania and the Preston-Webb ritual which was brought over and developed from England. There are different regional variations of the Preston-Webb ritual such as the ritual used by the Grand Lodge of Massachusetts.[184] However, some lodges in the USA still use the *Emulation Rite*—based on the Emulation Ritual under the UGLE. Prince Hall Freemasonry—predominantly African American Freemasonry—also gained recognition from the UGLE. In the Grand Lodge of Canada, Emulation Type Ritual is used.

What is the Eastern Star Masonic Organisation?

The Order of the Eastern Star was founded in the USA in 1850, and accepts both men and women; the men have to be Master Masons, and the women did, at one time, have to be related to the men in some way to join (wives, widows, sisters, or daughters), but now the Order accepts other female members from Orders such as the

Rainbow Girls. The International Order of the Rainbow for Girls are effectively a Masonic youth group, which was founded in the US in 1922, the Order being based on Masonic principles, the girls serving their community and becoming involved in charitable and educational projects. There is also another Masonic organisation called Job's Daughters, which are allowed to join the Eastern Star.

Is it true that lodges in the US can meet outside?

Yes, it is more common in rural areas, but there are lodges that meet on ranches, hilltops, caves, and in other outside areas, and actually confer degrees and conduct ceremonies. Some outside meetings have become traditional for certain lodges, such as the Castle Lodge No. 122, in Eagle, Colorado, which meets outside on a private ranch annually during the summer.[185] There is also a lodge in Montana, which still meets outside and has Tyler's mounted on horseback, with custom-made aprons for the horses!

There are many traditional outside meeting places for Masonic lodges in the US; one of the more famous examples being Independence Rock, in central Wyoming, which was a landmark and way-station on the old Oregon Trail, and became the first meeting place for Freemasons in what was to become the State of Wyoming. A similar site exists in Montana at the summit of Mullan Pass, which was the first recorded meeting place of Freemasons in the State in 1862. A stone alter and stone Officer's stations have been erected there.[186] In Indiana, a rock quarry was used as a meeting place for eighteen hundred Masons in 1967, using forty-five Tylers positioned around the rim of the quarry, and at a quarry in Marietta, Ohio, Tylers on horseback shouted from the rim of the quarry to report. Caves are also a common meeting place for lodges in the US, for example, in Kentucky, Masons met in Mammoth Cave, in Oregon, Malheur Cave has been the site of meetings of the Robert Burns Lodge No. 97,[187] and in New Mexico the Carlsbad Caverns have also witnessed lodge meetings.[188]

In England, for a lodge to meet outside is now unheard of, but there was a lodge under the Grand Lodge of Wigan that did meet under a bridge by the Leeds and Liverpool Canal near Wigan. This particular lodge called the Rose Bridge Lodge, was quite short lived, but was an interesting reminder that lodges could once meet this way. Apparently the lodge posted a Tyler at either end of the canal towpath to keep out intruders.[189] Meeting outside, under the sun, the moon and the stars, is for a lodge to meet under the active, natural Universe itself, and as long as the weather is good, there would be no place better.

Here is an example of Freemasons working in an outdoor lodge, wearing casual clothes and hats. It shows Past Grand Master of Arizona Brooke Cunningham (in white) delivering the Travelling Charge at COAZ outdoor lodge at the TNT Ranch, Gypsum, Colorado, (Castle Lodge No.122, AF&AM of Colorado). *Photograph by David Moran.*

Can Freemasons in the US wear casual clothes to the lodge?

Yes, there are lodges, especially in western states (such as Colorado, Arizona, New Mexico), which allow the wearing of casual clothes—jeans, denim shirts and boots for example, and of course, casual clothes are worn by Masons that meet in the aforementioned outside locations. This is because a number of lodge members in the more rural western states are agricultural workers, ranchers and farmers, and they may travel tens or

hundreds of miles to attend their lodge. Thus, their styles of clothes are traditional for them, and their lodges are traditionally built to accommodate this.[190] This seems to be the case in the nineteenth century; with the expansion westward, Freemasons sometimes met in their everyday working clothes, and evidence for this can be seen in photos of the period.

Why do Worshipful Masters in US lodges still wear hats?

In the US, unlike the UK, a hat is worn by the Worshipful Master to symbolise his authority, rank and status, and follows the tradition of the crown worn by King Solomon. The origins of the Worshipful Master wearing a hat can be traced back to the eighteenth century, and can be seen in various eighteenth and nineteenth century prints, which display Mason's working in the lodge and the Master wearing a tri-corn hat; the Grand Master of Massachusetts still wears a tri-corn hat. While Masonic hats differ within the various jurisdictions around the world, Masonic hats are a visible and somewhat traditional symbol of the Master's authority, and as such, equally reflect the hat to be of a respectful, classic or traditional style. Prince Hall Mason's for example, wear a white top hat, black top hat or a white fedora.

The hats worn by the Masters in the US vary, from a top hat or 'bowler' style, made from typical old school Beaver or silk, to a Stetson or western style hat in many of the western states. There is of course much 'doffing' of the hat during the ceremony, but the continuation of the Master wearing a hat in the US is a direct link to a Masonic past, which has since disappeared in the UK and most European countries.

Master's Hat, North Reading Lodge, MA

Aprons, North Reading Lodge, MA

Do Australian lodges wear informal dress and meet outside like US lodges?

Australia is in many ways, as formal and as traditional as the UK; it generally uses the Emulation Ritual (though with some small variations), has strict dress codes (generally black bow tie and dinner jacket), and it has six Grand lodges:

Grand Lodge of Western Australia

Grand Lodge of South Australia & Northern Territory

Grand Lodge of Tasmania

UGL of Victoria

UGL of New South Wales and the Australian Capital Territory

UGL of Queensland

There are a small number of lodges, (perhaps twenty or so) that use variations of Scottish rituals, and there are also nine lodges in the District Grand Lodge of Western Australia who are still under the Grand Lodge of Scotland and use nineteenth century Scottish rituals.

Meeting outside is very rare in Australia. One New South Wales lodge has met a couple of times in a large cave, and there is a Mark Lodge, which has met in a quarry in Australia. The quarry had supplied the stone for the Grand Lodge building in Brisbane.

On the 18th May 2013, the J W Jackson Lodge of Mark Master Masons No.32 on the Roll of the Grand Lodge of Mark Master Masons of Queensland, held an Advancement to the degree of Mark Master in the quarry at Yangan, north-east of Warwick, Queensland. This is the same quarry that provided sandstone for the Ann Street Masonic Memorial Temple, Home of the UGLQ. This Mark Lodge is named after James Watkin Jackson, a pioneer of Freemasonry in Queensland. He was the founding Master of North Australian Lodge No1 UGLQ, consecrated 13thJuly 1859, six months before the state of Queensland was proclaimed.
Photograph by David Cook.

With regards to dress Australian lodges are always formal. Dinner suits and bow ties are standard. In Queensland during the warmer months (October to March) white Eton Jackets (military mess jackets) are worn as an option. A dark suit and tie is perfectly acceptable for new brothers and visitors. Unlike the USA however, no hats are worn by the Worshipful Master (or any other Brethren) in Australian Craft lodges.[191]

How do New Zealand lodges meet?

New Zealand, on the whole, is similar to the Freemasonry practised in Australia, and has similar dress codes and ritual, though in the rural farming areas, dress codes differ and are more relaxed. Originally there were lodges founded under the English, Scottish and Irish Constitutions, but there was a strong movement in the 1870s and 1880s for a more centralised civil government, and Freemasonry followed suit. Thus in 1890, the Grand Lodge of New Zealand was formed to which most lodges affiliated, the rest remaining

English, Irish and Scottish. The New Zealand ritual began in 1903, although some older lodges use rituals from the English, Scottish or Irish Constitutions. However, due to cross membership and visiting, variations and 'cross-fertilisation' of ritual does occur.[192]

How do Canadian lodges meet?

Canadian lodges like the UK, Australia and New Zealand lodges, always attend in formal dress and in general, use Emulation type Ritual, though like Australia, there are lodges that use variations of the Scottish ritual. In some lodges, the Officers wear Tuxedos and the rest of the members, or visitors, usually wear a dark suit. There is a lodge that, like the one known in Australia, does meet outside once during the summer months. This outside way of meeting does seem more common, more traditional and more numerous in the US.[193]

Prominent Freemasons

How many US Presidents were Freemasons?

According to some books and conspiracy websites, an exceedingly long list of US Presidents have been put forward as being members of the Craft, George W. Bush being a much discussed Freemason on certain websites, when in fact he was never a Freemason; he was, like his father, a member of the Skull and Bones Society while at Yale and he planned to take his public oath of office on the George Washington Masonic Bible which belongs to the St. John's Lodge in New York, though due to rain another Bible was used. Other Presidents who also took their oath of office on the George Washington Bible include Jimmy Carter.

Here is a list of US Presidents who were Freemasons, fourteen in total:

George Washington
James Monroe
Andrew Jackson
James Polk
James Buchanan
Andrew Johnson
James Garfield
William McKinley
Theodore Roosevelt
Howard Taft
Warren Harding
Franklin Roosevelt
Harry Truman
Gerald Ford

Of the other Presidents who were linked to Freemasonry; Thomas Jefferson was not a Freemason, though he had attended a Masonic ceremony for laying the foundation stone and had many friends who were. Abraham Lincoln put his application to become a Freemason on hold while he took office, with the hope to resume his application after his office was over. Lyndon Johnson did take the First Degree in 1937, but did not pursue other degrees as his congressional duties took precedence. Ronald Reagan was an honorary member of the Imperial Temple of the Shrine and was involved in numerous Shrine and Masonic functions, but was not a Freemason.

Was Lord Nelson a Freemason?

Lord Nelson's Masonic membership has been much debated over the years. There is no firm evidence that he was a Freemason, though there is slight circumstantial evidence that he was considered a Mason during his lifetime. Freemasonry has attracted a large number of prominent men throughout the modern era, below are a few of the more historical Freemasons from Great Britain and the USA.

Some Famous British Freemasons:

The Duke of Wellington, commander, politician.

Sir Thomas Stamford Raffles, employee for the East India Company, assisting in establishing Freemasonry in Singapore.

Sir Winston Churchill, politician, historian and artist.

Rudyard Kipling, author of The Jungle Book, Kim, and poet.

Henry Rider Haggard, author of She, King Solomon's Mines.

Sir Arthur Conan Doyle, author of the Sherlock Holmes novels.

Branwell Brontë, poet, and ill-fated brother of the Brontë sisters.

Dr William John Polidori, Gothic writer and associate of Lord Byron.

Robbie Burns, poet.

Sir Walter Scott, writer of many popular novels, such as The Antiquary.

William Hogarth, engraver.

Oscar Wilde, writer and playwright.

Aleister Crowley, writer and occultist.

Edward Jenner, scientist, developed the vaccination for smallpox.

Alexander Fleming, biologist, discovered penicillin.

James Watt, engineer.

Some Famous US Freemasons:

Benjamin Franklin, writer, politician.

Paul Revere, silversmith and patriot in the American Revolution.

James Bowie, defender of the Alamo, inventor of the Bowie knife.

Davy Crockett, frontiersman, politician, and defender of the Alamo, Texas.

William B Travis, lawyer, commander, defender of the Alamo, Texas.

Sam Houston, politician, commander.

Mark Twain, author of The Adventures of Tom Sawyer and The Adventures of Huckleberry Finn.

John Wayne, actor (who once played Davy Crockett in the classic film version of The Alamo).

Oliver Hardy, actor, comedian.

Ernest Borgnine, actor.

Royal Freemasons:

Prince Frederick, Prince of Wales.

George IV (Grand Master of the 'Moderns').

William IV.

The Duke of Sussex (First Grand Master of the United Grand Lodge 1813-)

The Duke of Kent (Grand Master of the 'Antients' 1813).

Edward VII.

Edward VIII.

George VI.

The Duke of Kent (Grand Master of the United Grand Lodge 1966-).

Prince Michael of Kent.

The Duke of Edinburgh.

Endnotes

1   Kenneth Mackenzie, *The Royal Masonic Cyclopaedia*, (Worcester: The Aquarian Press, 1987), p.686.

2   See the Emulation Ritual, (Surrey: Lewis Masonic, 1995), pp.147-148.

3   Kenneth Mackenzie, *The Royal Masonic Cyclopaedia*, (Worcester: The Aquarian Press, 1987), pp. 240-241.

4   David Harrison, *The Transformation of Freemasonry*, (Bury St. Edmunds: Arima Publishing, 2010), pp.19-36.

5   Neville Barker Cryer, *York Mysteries Revealed*, (Hersham: Barker Cryer, 2006), pp.221-222.

6   See http://www.ugle.org.uk/what-is-masonry/frequently-asked-questions/ [accessed on the 7th of February, 2013]

7   See David Harrison, *The Genesis of Freemasonry*, (Hersham: Lewis Masonic, 2009), pp.10-11.

8   Kenneth Mackenzie, *The Royal Masonic Cyclopaedia*, (Worcester: The Aquarian Press, 1987), pp. 450-451.

9   Arthur Edward Waite, *A New Encyclopaedia of Freemasonry*, Vol I., (New York: Wings Books, 1996), pp.152-153.

10   Kenneth Mackenzie, *The Royal Masonic Cyclopaedia*, (Worcester: The Aquarian Press, 1987), pp.136-137.

11   See the Emulation Ritual, (Surrey: Lewis Masonic, 1995), p.37.

12   See F.R. Worts, 'The Apron and its Symbolism', *AQC*, Vol. 74, (1961).

13   See William Morgan, *Illustrations of Masonry By One Of The Fraternity Who has Devoted Thirty Years to the Subject*, (Batavia, New York: David C. Miller, 1827). Also see Richard Carlile, *Manual of Freemasonry*, (London: William Reeves, 1912), p.87.

14   See David Harrison, *The Liverpool Masonic Rebellion and the Wigan Grand Lodge*, (Bury St. Edmunds: Arima Publishing, 2012), p.49.

15   Minutes of the Lodge of Lights No. 148, Warrington Masonic Hall, *July, 1797*. Not listed.

16   Ibid., *March 1803*.

17   Ibid., *1804-1805*.

18   See Stephen Knight, *The Brotherhood; The Secret World of the Freemasons*, (London: Book Club Associates, 1984), in which Knight sensationally puts forward various stories of how the police, barristers, judges and solicitors, have supposedly used Freemasonry in England and Wales for promotion and to pervert the course of justice. Knight discussed how he used 'moles' within Freemasonry to expose these stories, but it has a severe lack of references and the names of these 'moles' are never revealed. The work became an extremely popular book, though Knight died soon after.

19 BBC UK: Politics 'New Judges Must Declare Masonic Membership', Thursday, March 5, 1998, http://news.bbc.co.uk/1/hi/uk/politics/57381.stm [accessed 17th of October, 2012]. Jack Straw was the Home Secretary from 1997 to 2001 under the Labour Government.

20 Anon., *Jachin and Boaz, a New Edition*, (London: W. Nicoll, 1785), p.9.

21 Some London based clubs now accept women as members, such as the Reform Club, Athenaeum Club and the Carlton Club. Also see David Harrison, *The Transformation of Freemasonry*, (Bury St. Edmunds: Arima Publishing, 2010), pp.157-162.

22 See Philippa Faulks & Cheryl Skidmore, *A Handbook for the Freemason's Wife*, (Hersham: Lewis Masonic, 2009).

23 See the Emulation Ritual, (Surrey: Lewis Masonic, 1995), p.68.

24 See the *Constitutions of the Antient Fraternity of Free & Accepted Masons under the United Grand Lodge of England*, (London: Freemasons Hall, 1919), pp.6, and see also the *UGLE Book of Constitutions*, (London: Freemason' Hall, 1989), p.5.

25 See the UGLE Universities Scheme; http://www.ugle.org.uk/how-to-become-a-mason/university-section/ [accessed 17th of October, 2012]

26 *Emulation Ritual*, (Surrey: Lewis Masonic, 1996), p.100.

27 See Harrison, *Transformation of Freemasonry*, pp.12-15.

28 See Harrison, *The Liverpool Masonic Rebellion and the Wigan Grand Lodge*, p.57.

29 The Halliwell Manuscript, Lines 427-434, No. 17, A1, British Museum.

30 Anon., *Jachin and Boaz, a New Edition*, (London: W. Nicoll, 1785), p.9, and Anon., *Three Distinct Knocks, Seventh Edition*, (London: H. Serjeant, 1775), p.15.

31 Della Thompson (ed.), *The Oxford Compact English Dictionary*, (Oxford: Oxford University Press, 1996), p.685 and p.686.

32 *Emulation Ritual, Revised Edition*, (Surrey: Lewis Masonic, 1996), p.75.

33 Anon., *Jachin and Boaz, a New Edition*, (London: W. Nicoll, 1785), pp.9-10.

34 Anon., *Three Distinct Knocks, Seventh Edition*, (London: H. Serjeant, 1775), pp.15-16.

35 Harrison, *Transformation of Freemasonry*, pp.12-13.

36 Richard Carlile, *Manual of Freemasonry*, (London: William Reeves, 1912), p.7.

37 The New English Bible, (Oxford: Oxford University Press, 1970), p.336.

38 *Emulation Ritual*, (Surrey: Lewis Masonic, 1996), p.183.

39 See David Harrison, 'The Lymm Freemasons; A New Insight into Transition-Era Freemasonry', in *Heredom*, Vol. 19, (Washington: Scottish Rite Research Society, 2011), pp.169-190.

40 See Harrison, *Genesis of Freemasonry*, pp.26-27.

41   See Harrison, *Genesis of Freemasonry*, pp.149-161.

42   See Robert Cooper, *The Roslyn Hoax*, (Hersham: Lewis Masonic, 2009).

43   For more information on the development of the Masonic Knights Templar Order, see Harrison, *Transformation of Freemasonry*, pp.143-156.

44   See http://www.redcrossofconstantine.co.uk/history.html [accessed 16th of November, 2012]

45   See J. Fairbairn Smith, 'Did Shakespeare Create Masonic Ritual?', in *Fiat Lux*, (Philalethes Society, 2009), pp.231-236.

46   See *The Illustrated Stratford Shakespeare*, (London: Chancellor Press, 1992), p.88.

47   Ibid., p.260.

48   Ibid., p.72.

49   See Harrison, *Genesis of Freemasonry*, pp.89-90.

50   Ibid., p.76.

51   See Rev. A.F.A Woodford, 'Freemasonry and Hermeticisim', and W.W. Westcott, 'The Religion of Freemasonry illuminated by the Kabbalah', in *AQC*, Vol. 1, (1888), pp.28-36 and pp.55-59.

52   R.F. Gould, 'English Freemasonry Before the Era of Grand Lodge', in *AQC*, Vol. 1, (1888), pp.67-74.

53   See Robert A. Gilbert, 'Masonic Education: Leading the way', in *MQ, Grand Lodge Publications, Issue 11, October, 2004.*

54   See Harrison, *Transformation of Freemasonry*, pp.49-50.

55   Arthur Wellesley, The Duke of Wellington, was initiated into his family lodge Trim No. 494, in Ireland, on the 7th of December, 1790, his father and brother both serving as Worshipful Master of the lodge and both serving as Grand Master of the Grand Lodge of Ireland. Wellington had been elected as MP for Trim that same year, and seemed to abandon Freemasonry around 1795 after he had entered the military. On his death in 1852, his friend Viscount Combermere, who was Provincial Grand Master for Cheshire, gave a speech to the Provincial Grand Lodge regarding Wellington's links to Freemasonry. See Harrison, *Transformation of Freemasonry*, pp.81-82.

56   The *Guardian*, Saturday 28th of March, 1829, http://www.guardian.co.uk/news/1829/mar/28/mainsection.fromthearchive [accessed 8th of December, 2012]

57   Alexander Pushkin was a member of Lodge Ovid, Kischinev, joining in 1821.

58   George L. Marshall, 'Brother Albert Pike's Duel', in *Knight Templar Magazine*, Vol. LVIII, No. 2, (February 2012), pp.10-13.

59   Andrew Jackson was a member of Harmony Lodge No. 1, Tennessee, by 1800, and he served as Grand Master of Tennessee from 1822-1824. His Masonic apron is on display at the Tennessee State Museum. See also Fred O. Wyant, 'Dueling Masons' http://www.masonic.benemerito.net/msricf/papers/wyant/wyant-dueling_masons.pdf [accessed 12th of

60 *Minute book of the Lodge of Lights No. 148, 2nd of May, 1806.* Warrington Masonic Hall.

61 Harrison, *The Liverpool Masonic Rebellion and the Wigan Grand Lodge,* p.66.

62 Elias Ashmole, *The Diary and Will of Elias Ashmole,* (Oxford: Butler & Tanner, 1927), p.26.

63 See Harrison, *Genesis of Freemasonry.*

64 T.W. Hanson, *The Lodge of Probity No. 61 1738-1938,* (Halifax: Lodge of Probity, 1939), pp.189-216.

65 This was certainly not uncommon; the Lodge of Probity in Halifax, Yorkshire, also has evidence that it conducted its ritual around a table during the later eighteenth century. See the eighteenth century print in this book.

66 See Harrison, *The Liverpool Masonic Rebellion and the Wigan Grand Lodge.*

67 For the flexibility of the Masonic ritual within the Scottish Rite, see C. DeForrest Trexler, 'The Degree Rituals of the Northern Masonic Jurisdiction', *Heredom,* Vol. 17, (2009), pp.125-198, http://scottishrite.org/wp-content/uploads/2010/12/heredom_v17_rituals.pdf [accessed 5th of September, 2012]

68 *Emulation Ritual,* (Surrey: Lewis Masonic, 1996), pp.8-9. See also Harrison, *Genesis of Freemasonry,* p.43.

69 See Rule 181 referring to Private Lodges in the *Constitutions of the Antient Fraternity of Free & Accepted Masons under the United Grand Lodge of England,* (London:

Freemasons Hall, 1919), p.92. See also Harrison, *The Liverpool Masonic Rebellion and the Wigan Grand Lodge,* pp.84.

70 See Harrison, *The Liverpool Masonic Rebellion and the Wigan Grand Lodge,* pp.83-86.

71 Llewellyn Kitchen, (ed.), *A Ritual of Craft Masonry "Humber Use",* (Hull: Privately Published, 1988).

72 See Michael Barnes, 'Spoilt for Choice', *MQ,* Issue 10, (July, 2004), http://www.mqmagazine.co.uk/issue-10/p-62.php [accessed on the 16th of January, 2012]

73 The Merchant Lodge has its own privately printed ritual book, and has variations on the Emulation ritual.

74 Many of these rituals can still be obtained such as Taylor's and Stability, and some are still privately printed such as the Bottomley and Humber rituals. See also Anon., *West End Ritual of Craft Masonry,* (Hersham: Lewis Masonic, 2011) and Anon., *M.M. Taylor's First Degree Handbook of Craft Freemasonry,* (Hersham: Lewis Masonic, 2006).

75 All these rituals are still available from the Grand Lodge of Scotland. Many thanks to Kenneth Jack of Lodge St. Andrew No. 814, for his information on Scottish rituals and various Scottish lodge Working. Lodge St Andrew uses the Harvey ritual with local variations.

76 The Halliwell Manuscript, Line 793, No. 17, A1, British Museum.

77 Harrison, *Transformation of Freemasonry,* p.166.

78 *Emulation Ritual, Revised Edition*, (Surrey: Lewis Masonic, 1996), p.64.

79 See the *Constitutions of the Antient Fraternity of Free & Accepted Masons under the United Grand Lodge of England*, (London: Freemasons Hall, 1919), p.7.

80 See Harrison, *Genesis of Freemasonry*, pp.119-120.

81 *Emulation Ritual*, (Surrey: Lewis Masonic, 1996), pp.63. The Emulation ritual states that a 'report' is given at the beginning of the first degree ceremony, before the candidate enters the lodge, but many lodges change this and indicate the action as an 'alarm'.

82 Harrison, *Genesis of Freemasonry*, pp.127-128.

83 *Emulation Ritual*, (Surrey: Lewis Masonic, 1996), p.46.

84 Richard Carlile, *Manual of Freemasonry*, (London: William Reeves, 1912), p.111. In 'Complete Workings' and others, the question is put to the principal sojourner not Haggai.

85 Llewellyn Kitchen, (ed.), *A Ritual of Craft Masonry "Humber Use"*, (Hull: Privately Published, 1988), p.55.

86 Kenneth Mackenzie, *The Royal Masonic Cyclopaedia*, (Worcester: The Aquarian Press, 1987), p.171.

87 See Harrison, *Genesis of Freemasonry*, pp.18-19.

88 See Anon., *Three Distinct Knocks, Seventh Edition*, (London: H. Serjeant, 1775), p.29.

89 See Anon., *Jachin and Boaz, a New Edition*, (London: W. Nicoll, 1785), p.vi and p.7.

90 See the excellent Short Talk Bulletins on the website for the Grand Lodge of the state of Louisiana, USA: http://www.la-mason.com/stb52.htm [accessed 9th of February, 2013]

91 George Oliver, *The Book of the Lodge or Officer's Manual*, (London: R. Spencer, 1849), p.116.

92 James Anderson, *Constitutions of the Antient and Honourable Fraternity of Free and Accepted Masons*, (London: G. Kearsly, 1769), p.229.

93 T.W. Hanson, *The Lodge of Probity No. 61 1738-1938*, (Halifax: Lodge of Probity, 1939), pp.76-80.

94 See Harrison, *The Liverpool Masonic Rebellion and the Wigan Grand Lodge*, p.67.

95 Harrison, *Transformation of Freemasonry*, p.181.

96 See the *Constitutions of the Antient Fraternity of Free & Accepted Masons under the United Grand Lodge of England*, (London: Freemasons Hall, 1919), pp.148-154.

97 *Emulation Ritual*, (Surrey: Lewis Masonic, 1996), pp.94-95.

98 Ibid.

99 Ibid., pp.137-138.

100 Ibid., pp.252-253.

101 Ibid.

102 See Harrison, *The Liverpool Masonic Rebellion and the Wigan Grand Lodge*.

103 Philippa Faulks & Cheryl Skidmore, *A Handbook for the Freemason's Wife*, (Hersham: Lewis Masonic, 2009), p.51.

104 Freemasons' Monthly Magazine, Vol. XXIII, (Boston: Hugh H. Tuttle, 1864), p.158.

105 Liverpool Mercury, 13th of January, 1864, issue 4970, p.6.

106 See the history of the Riverside Lodge No. 4201, consecrated in 1921, http://www.phoenix3236.org.uk/riverside/history.html [accessed 23rd of November, 2012]

107 Anon., *Three Distinct Knocks*, (London, 1760), pp.11-12.

108 See Harry Carr, 'Masonic Fire', *AQC*, Vol. 79, (1966).

109 See Neville Barker Cryer, *Masonic Halls of England: The South*, (Hersham: Lewis Masonic, 1989), pp.13-14.

110 See Neville Barker Cryer, *Masonic Halls of England: The North*, (Hersham: Lewis Masonic, 1989), p.131 & p.135.

111 Anon., *Three Distinct Knocks*, pp.9-10. The diagram can be seen within this guide.

112 See Harrison, *Genesis of Freemasonry*, p.22.

113 See Fred Lomax, "Fower Nowt One' – Royal Forest Lodge No. 401 and the Waddington Stone', *The Square*, September 2012, pp.22-23. Also see The West Lancashire Masonic Year Book, 2011-12, (Liverpool: Province of West Lancashire, 2011), p.50.

114 See also Harry Carr, 'The Full Moon and Freemasonry', *AQC*, Vol. 80, (1967).

115 T.W. Hanson, *The Lodge of Probity No. 61 1738-1938*, (Halifax: Lodge of Probity, 1939), p.71.

116 Ibid., p.74.

117 Robert Leslie Wood, *York Lodge No. 236, 1777-1977*, (York, 1977), p.15.

118 W.B. Stephens, *Adult Education and Society in an Industrial Town: Warrington 1800-1900*, (Exeter: University of Exeter, 1980), p.81.

119 See the *Constitutions of the Antient Fraternity of Free & Accepted Masons under the United Grand Lodge of England*, (London: Freemasons Hall, 1919), p.97.

120 Ibid, p.98.

121 T.W. Hanson, *The Lodge of Probity No. 61 1738-1938*, (Halifax: Lodge of Probity, 1939), p.68.

122 See Harrison, *Genesis of Freemasonry*, p.93.

123 Anon., *UGLE Book of Constitutions*, (London: Freemason' Hall, 1989), p.108.

124 See Harrison, *Genesis of Freemasonry*, p.180.

125 Barker Cryer, *York Mysteries*, p.365.

126 Minutes of the Lodge of Lights, No.148, Warrington Masonic Hall, *19th of July, 1821*. Not listed. There is also a poster advertising the Coronation procession of George IV, held in St. Elphin's Church, Warrington, which states that the 'Free-Masons' were leading the procession.

127 Minutes of the Lodge of Lights, No.148, Warrington Masonic Hall, *22nd of December, 1836*. Not listed. The items are now on display at the Warrington Museum. See also Anon., *The History of The Lodge of Harmony No. 220*, (Liverpool, 1948), p.9.

128 John Armstrong, *A History of Freemasonry in Cheshire*, (London: Kenning, 1901), pp.110-111.

129 Philip Alexander Bruce. *History of the University of Virginia, 1819-1919*, (New York: Macmillan, 1920), pp.189-190.

130 See Chris Hodapp's website http://freemasonsfordummies.blogspot.co.uk/2011/08/grand-lodge-of-indiana-procession-last.html [accessed 25th of September, 2012]

131 Freemasonry Today, No. 19, Grand Lodge Publications Ltd., (Autumn, 2012), p.24.

132 Thanks to Lee Robert McStein who is a member of Lodge St Andrew No. 6, UGLQ, Australia.

133 Kenneth Mackenzie, *The Royal Masonic Cyclopaedia*, (Worcester: The Aquarian Press, 1987), p.707.

134 Barker Cryer, *Masonic Halls of England: The North*, pp.24-25.

135 Harrison, *Transformation of Freemasonry*, pp.67-68.

136 See the excellent website for the London based Mersey Lodge No. 5434 for further information: www.merseylodge5434.org/ [accessed 5th of October 2012]

137 David Stevenson, *The First Freemasons; Scotland's Early Lodges and their Members*, (Aberdeen: Aberdeen University Press, 1988), p.28. See also David Harrison, *Genesis of Freemasonry*, (Hersham: Lewis Masonic, 2009), p.26.

138 See Harrison, *Genesis of Freemasonry*, pp.48-49.

139 See George Oliver, *Signs and Symbols Illustrated and Explained in a Course of Twelve Lectures on Freemasonry*, (London: Sherwood, Gilbert and Piper, 1837).

140 Harrison, *Transformation of Freemasonry*, pp.165-6.

141 See Basil Willey, *The Seventeenth Century Background*, (London: Chatto & Windus, 1946), pp.210-213, which discusses Sprat's notable history of the Royal Society and how the Royal Society was formed.

142 See Sir Thomas Browne, *The Garden of Cyrus*, (London: 1658). Browne concludes his work with '*All things began in order, so shall they end, and so shall they begin again*'.

143 *Constitutions of the Antient Fraternity of Free and Accepted Masons under the United Grand Lodge of England*, (London: Freemason's Hall, 1989), p.181.

144 See Harrison, *The Liverpool Masonic Rebellion and the Wigan Grand Lodge*, p.63.

145 See Peter Jones, *The French Revolution in Social & Political Perspective*, (London: Arnold, 1996), pp.192-199.

146 *UGLE Book of Constitutions*, (London: Freemason' Hall, 1989), p.150.

147 See James Anderson, *The Constitutions of The Free-Masons*, (London: Senex, 1723). The frontispiece was by the engraver and Freemason John Pine.

148 Edward Dobson, *A Rudimentary Treatise on Masonry and Stonecutting*, (London: John Weale, 1849), p.35.

149 M. Gauding, *The Signs and Symbols Bible: The Definitive Guide to Mysterious Markings*, (London: Godsfield Press, 2009), p.87.

150 Edward Batley, 'Freemasonry, Literature and Society: Cultural

Reciprocity in the Pre-History of the Grand Lodge of London (1717)', in *Anglo-American Awareness: Arpeggios in Aesthetics*, (New Jersey: Transaction Publishers Rutgers University, 2005), pp.29-45, on p.34.

151 Della Thompson (ed.), *The Oxford Compact English Dictionary*, (Oxford: Oxford University Press, 1996), p.937.

152 Ibid., p.1001.

153 Ibid., p.1114.

154 See http://www.masonicforumoflight.com/PDFS/ORDERSPDF.pdf [accessed 31st of October, 2012]

155 See Harrison, *Transformation of Freemasonry*, pp.152-3.

156 See R.S.E., Sandbach, *Priest and Freemason: The Life of George Oliver*, (Northamptonshire: The Aquarian Press, 1988), p.108-109. For information on Dr Robert Thomas Crucefix see R.S.E., Sandbach, 'Robert Thomas Crucefix, 1788-1850', in *AQC*, Vol. 102, (1990), pp.134-163.

157 Albert Pike, *Morals and Dogma of the Ancient and Accepted Scottish Rite of Freemasonry*, (NuVision Publications LLC, 2007), p.186.

158 Ibid., pp.187-191.

159 George Oliver, *The Origin of the Royal Arch Order of Masonry*, (London: Bro. Richard Spencer, 1867), p.4.

160 For information on the Grand Lodge of York, see Harrison, *The Genesis of Freemasonry*, pp.181-189, and Barker Cryer, *York Mysteries Revealed.*

161 Malcolm C. Duncan, *Duncan's Masonic Ritual and Monitor*, (Forgotten Books, 2008), p.1.

162 See the excellent article by Douglas H. Wood, 'The Art of Memory and the Masonic Craft', in *Philalethes*, Vol. 65, No. 1, (2012), pp.6-15. Also see David Stevenson, *The Origins of Freemasonry: Scotland's Century, 1590-1710*, (Cambridge: Cambridge University Press, 1988), pages 34 and 43, where Stevenson discusses how the Art of Memory was used in Scottish lodges as early as the 1590s. The Revised Edition of the Emulation Ritual has been used, (Hersham: Lewis Masonic, 1995).

163 See Harrison, *Genesis of Freemasonry*, pp.54-55 and pp.134-5.

164 Ibid, pp.126-7.

165 See Sir Charles Warren, 'On the Orientation of Temples', in *AQC*, Vol. 1, (1888), pp.36-50.

166 See Harrison, *Transformation of Freemasonry*, pp.194-5.

167 See The New English Bible, (Oxford: Oxford University Press, 1970), p.379.

168 Ibid., p.479.

169 Harrison, *Genesis of Freemasonry*, p.55.

170 Anon., *Jachin and Boaz; or an Authentic Key To the Door of Free-Masonry, Both Antient and Modern*, (London: W. Nicoll, St. Paul's Church-Yard, 1763), p.47.

171 *Emulation Ritual*, (Surrey: Lewis Masonic, 1996), pp.194-5.

172 Kenneth Mackenzie, *The Royal Masonic Cyclopaedia*, (Worcester: The Aquarian Press, 1987), pp.507-8.

173 Harrison, *Genesis of Freemasonry*, p.123.

174 See Harrison, *Transformation of Freemasonry*, pp.194-5.

175 Della Thompson (ed.), *The Oxford Compact English Dictionary*, (Oxford: Oxford University Press, 1996), p.688.

176 See Harrison, *Transformation of Freemasonry*, pp.162-170.

177 See David Harrison, 'From Elias Ashmole to Arthur Edward Waite', *Philalethes*, Volume 64, No. 1, (Winter 2011), pp.21-29.

178 Mackenzie, *The Royal Masonic Cyclopaedia*, p.701.

179 Neville Barker-Cryer, *Masonic Halls of England: The North*, (Hersham: Lewis Masonic, 1989), p.97. Examples of Officers chairs showing the rising Sun over the Worshipful Masters chair, the Sun over the Junior Warden's chair, and the Moon over the Senior Warden's chair can be seen in Sunderland Masonic Hall. The chairs were purchased in 1784.

180 See Tim Fulford, *Romantic Indians: Native Americans, British Literature, and Transatlantic Culture 1756-1830*, (Oxford: Oxford University Press, 2006). Fulford discusses how Native North American Indians and British colonists had a closer relationship during this period and how they influenced each other in literature and culture. Also see Harrison, *Transformation of Freemasonry*, pp.186-8.

181 See Allen E. Roberts, *House Undivided: The Story of Freemasonry and the Civil War*, (Missouri, USA: Missouri Lodge of Research, 1961). Also see Joseph Fort Newton, *The Builders*, (London: Unwin Brothers Limited, 1924).

182 Brigadier General Lewis Addison Armistead, originally from North Carolina, was a member of Alexandria-Washington Masonic Lodge No. 22, and before the Civil War he had served with his friend and fellow Mason Major General Winfield Scott Hancock, who was a member of Charity Lodge No. 190. Captain Henry H. Bingham, serving under Hancock at Gettysburg, was a member of Chartiers Lodge No. 297. See also David Harrison, *The Transformation of Freemasonry*, (Bury St. Edmunds: Arima Publishing, 2010), p.118.

183 See http://www.halcyontemple.org/about/ [accessed 15th of February, 2013]

184 *Official Cipher*, (Boston: Grand Lodge of Masons in Massachusetts, 2002). This is the official ritual book for the lodges under the Grand Lodge of Massachusetts.

185 The Castle Lodge No. 122 in Eagle, Colorado, hosts the outdoor lodge event annually with permission of the Colorado Grand Lodge AF&AM. It is put on at Bro. Larry Trotter's TNT Ranch outside of Gypsum Colorado named 'COAZ'.

186 For the history of the Mullan Pass Historic Lodge No. 1862 which presently meets on the historic site, see http://www.helenamasons.org/MullanPass05.htm [accessed on the 30th of December, 2012]

187 For the history of the Robert Burns

Lodge No. 97 and the Malheur Cave, see http://www.burnslodge.org/malheur.html [accessed on the 30th of December, 2012]

188 K. Arrington, 'Highest Hills or Lowest Vales', www.masonicworld.com [accessed on the 30th of December, 2012]

189 See Harrison, *The Liverpool Masonic Rebellion and the Wigan Grand Lodge*, p.59. In England, Pseudo Masonic clubs, such as the Hell Fire Club, also known as the Monks of Medmenham, certainly met in caves on the estate of Sir Francis Dashwood in West Wycombe during the mid-eighteenth century, and it has been suggested that the cave-like tunnels of Joseph Williamson in Liverpool, constructed in the early nineteenth century, were used as a meeting place of some sorts, but there is no evidence for Masonic meetings in caves in England. See Harrison, *Genesis of Freemasonry*, pp.139-141. There have been religious gatherings held outside in England, such as the Primitive Methodist meetings of the early nineteenth century held at Mow Cop, the rugged outcrop that straddles the border of Cheshire and Staffordshire, and more recently, the New Age gatherings of Stone Henge during the Summer and Winter Solstice, though in the US, especially in the western States and rural areas of the south, it was common to hold religious meetings outside and conduct baptisms in rivers.

190 Many thanks to various US Masons for their descriptions of how their lodges operate, and special thanks to David Moran from Elk Mountain Lodge, No. 118, Steamboat Springs, Colorado, for his descriptions of outdoor lodges and rules on dress while at the lodges.

191 Many thanks to David Cook for his information on Australian lodges. David Cook is a member of Barron Barnett Lodge of Research No. 146, United Grand Lodge of Queensland.

192 Many thanks to Alan Bevin for his information on New Zealand lodges.

193 Many thanks to Dave Lauretti for his information on Canadian lodges. Dave Lauretti is a member of Burlington Lodge No. 165.

Bibliography

Anderson, James, *The Constitutions of The Free-Masons*, (London: Senex, 1723).

Anderson, James, *The New Book of Constitutions of the Antient and Honourable Fraternity of Free and Accepted Masons*, (London: Ward and Chandler, 1738).

Anderson, James, *The Constitutions of the Antient and Honourable Fraternity of Free and Accepted Masons, Revised by John Entick MA*, (London: J. Scott, 1756).

Anderson, James, *Constitutions of the Antient and Honourable Fraternity of Free and Accepted Masons*, (London: G. Kearsly, 1769).

Anon., *Three Distinct Knocks*, (London, 1760).

Anon., *Jachin and Boaz; or an Authentic Key To the Door of Free-Masonry, Both Antient and Modern*, (London: W. Nicoll, St. Paul's Church-Yard, 1763).

Anon., *The Life of Captain Joseph Brant with An Account of his Re-interment at Mohawk, 1850, and of the Corner Stone Ceremony in the Erection of the Brant Memorial, 1886*, (Ontario, Brantford: B.H. Rothwell, 1886).

Anon., *Constitutions of the Antient Fraternity of Free & Accepted Masons under the United Grand Lodge of England*, (London: Freemasons Hall, 1919).

Anon., *The History of The Lodge of Harmony No. 220*, (Liverpool, 1948).

Anon., *Emulation Ritual*, (Surrey: Lewis Masonic, 1996).

Anon., *The West Lancashire Masonic Year Book, 2011-12*, (Liverpool: Province of West Lancashire, 2011).

Anon., *M.M. Taylor's First Degree Handbook of Craft Freemasonry*, (Hersham: Lewis Masonic, 2006).

Anon., *West End Ritual of Craft Masonry*, (Hersham: Lewis Masonic, 2011).

Armstrong, John, *A History of Freemasonry in Cheshire*, (London: Kenning, 1901).

Ashmole, Elias, *The Diary and Will of Elias Ashmole*, (Oxford: Butler & Tanner, 1927).

Barker Cryer, Neville, *Masonic Halls of England: The South*, (Hersham: Lewis Masonic, 1989).

Barker Cryer, Neville, *Masonic Halls of England: The North*, (Hersham: Lewis Masonic, 1989).

Barker Cryer, Neville, *York Mysteries Revealed*, (Hersham: Barker-Cryer, 2006).

Browne, Sir Thomas, *The Garden of Cyrus*, (London: 1658).

Bruce, Philip Alexander, *History of the University of Virginia, 1819-1919*, (New York: Macmillan, 1920).

Carlile, Richard, *Manual of Freemasonry*, (Croydon: New Temple Press, 1912).

Carr, Harry, *The Freemason at Work*, (London: Burgess & Sons, 1976).

Cooper, Robert, *The Roslyn Hoax*, (Hersham: Lewis Masonic, 2009).

Dermott, Laurence, *Ahiman Rezon*, (London, 1756).

Dermott, Laurence, *Ahiman Rezon, or a help to all that are, or would be Free and Accepted Masons, Second Edition*, (London: Sold by Br. Robert Black, 1764).

Dermott, Laurence, *Ahiman Rezon or a Help to all that are, or would be Free and Accepted Masons (with many additions), Third Edition*, (London: Printed for James Jones, 1778).

A Quick Guide To Freemasonry

Dobson, Edward, *A Rudimentary Treatise on Masonry and Stonecutting,* (London: John Weale, 1849).

Duncan, Malcolm C., *Duncan's Masonic Ritual and Monitor,* (Forgotten Books, 2008).

Eliot C.W., (ed.), *The Autobiography of Benjamin Franklin,* (New York: P.F. Collier and Son, 1909).

Faulks, Philippa, & Skidmore, Cheryl, *A Handbook for the Freemason's Wife,* (Hersham: Lewis Masonic, 2009).

Fort Newton, Joseph, *The Builders,* (London: Unwin Brothers Limited, 1924).

Fulford, Tim, *Romantic Indians: Native Americans, British Literature, and Transatlantic Culture 1756-1830,* (Oxford: Oxford University Press, 2006).

Franklin, Benjamin, *The Autobiography of Benjamin Franklin,* (New York: Courier Dover Publications, 1996).

Gauding, M., *The Signs and Symbols Bible: The Definitive Guide to Mysterious Markings,* (London: Godsfield Press, 2009).

Gould, R.F., *The History of Freemasonry, Vol. I-VI,* (London, 1884-7).

Hanson, T.W., *The Lodge of Probity No. 61 1738-1938,* (Halifax: Lodge of Probity, 1939).

Harrison, David, *The Genesis of Freemasonry,* (Hersham: Lewis Masonic, 2009).

Harrison David, *The Transformation of Freemasonry,* (Bury St. Edmunds: Arima Publishing, 2010).

Harrison David, *The Liverpool Masonic Rebellion and the Wigan Grand Lodge,* (Bury St. Edmunds: Arima Publishing, 2012).

Hutchinson, William, *The Spirit of masonry in moral and elucidatory lectures,* (London: printed for J. Wilkie and W. Goldsmith, 1775).

Jones, Peter, *The French Revolution in Social & Political Perspective,* (London: Arnold, 1996).

Jonson, Ben, *The Works of Ben Jonson,* (New York: G. and W. Nicol, 1816).

Jonson, Ben, *Selected Poetry,* (London: Penguin, 1992).

Josten, C.H., (ed.), *Elias Ashmole 1617-1692. His autobiographical and historical notes, his correspondence and other contemporary sources relating to his life and work,* (Oxford: Oxford University Press, 1966).

Kitchen, Llewellyn, (ed.), *A Ritual of Craft Masonry "Humber Use",* (Hull: Privately Published, 1988).

Knoop, D., *On the Connection between Operative and Speculative Masonry,* (London: AQC, 1935).

Knoop, D., and Jones, G.P., *A Short History of Freemasonry To 1730,* (Manchester: University of Manchester Press, 1940).

Knoop, D., *Freemasonry and the Idea of Natural Religion,* (London: Butler & Tanner, 1942).

Knoop, D., and Jones, G.P., (ed.), *Early Masonic Pamphlets,* (Manchester: University of Manchester Press, 1945).

Knoop, D., and Jones, G.P., *The Mediaeval Mason: An Economic History of English Stone Building in the Later Middle Ages and Early Modern Times,* (New York: Barnes and Noble, 1967).

Knight, Stephen, *The Brotherhood: The Secret World of the Freemasons,* (London: Book Club Associates, 1984).

Mackenzie, Kenneth, *The Royal Masonic

Cyclopaedia, (Worcester: The Aquarian Press, 1987).

Morgan, William, *Illustrations of Masonry By One Of The Fraternity Who has Devoted Thirty Years to the Subject*, (Batavia, New York: David C. Miller, 1827).

Oliver, George, *Signs and Symbols Illustrated and Explained in a Course of Twelve Lectures on Freemasonry*, (London: Sherwood, Gilbert and Piper, 1837).

Oliver, George, *The Book of the Lodge or Officer's Manual*, (London: R. Spencer, 1849).

Oliver, George, *The Origin of the Royal Arch Order of Masonry*, (London: Bro. Richard Spencer, 1867).

Paine, Thomas, *The Works of Thomas Paine*, (New York: E. Haskell, 1854).

Pike, Albert, *Morals and Dogma of the Ancient and Accepted Scottish Rite of Freemasonry*, (NuVision Publications LLC, 2007).

Plot, Robert, *Natural History of Staffordshire*, (Oxford, 1686).

Preston, William, *Illustrations of Masonry*, (London: Whittaker, Treacher & co., 1829).

Prichard, Samuel, *Tubal-Kain*, (London: W. Nicoll, 1760).

Roberts, Allen E., *House Undivided: The Story of Freemasonry and the Civil War*, (Missouri, USA: Missouri Lodge of Research, 1961).

Sandbach, R.S.E., *Priest and Freemason: The Life of George Oliver*, (Northamptonshire: The Aquarian Press, 1988).

Shakespear, William, *The Illustrated Stratford Shakespeare*, (London: Chancellor Press, 1992).

Stephens, W.B., *Adult Education and Society in an Industrial Town: Warrington 1800-1900*, (Exeter: University of Exeter, 1980).

Stevenson, David, *The Origins of Freemasonry: Scotland's Century, 1590-1710*, (Cambridge: Cambridge University Press, 1988).

Stevenson, David, *The First Freemasons; Scotland's Early Lodges and their Members*, (Aberdeen: Aberdeen University Press, 1988).

Waite, A.E., *A New Encyclopaedia of Freemasonry*, Vol. I & II, (New York: Wings Books Edition, 1996).

Willey, Basil, *The Seventeenth Century Background*, (London: Chatto & Windus, 1946).

Wood, Robert Leslie, *York Lodge No. 236, 1777-1977*, (York, 1977).

Journals

Batley, Edward, 'Freemasonry, Literature and Society: Cultural Reciprocity in the Pre-History of the Grand Lodge of London (1717)', in *Anglo-American Awareness: Arpeggios in Aesthetics*, (New Jersey: Transaction Publishers Rutgers University, 2005), pp.29-45.

DeForrest Trexler, C., 'The Degree Rituals of the Northern Masonic Jurisdiction', *Heredom*, Vol. 17, (2009), pp.125-198.

Fairbairn Smith, J., 'Did Shakespeare Create Masonic Ritual?', in *Fiat Lux*, (Philalethes Society, 2009), pp.231-236.

Gould, R.F., 'English Freemasonry Before the Era of Grand Lodge', in *AQC*, Vol. 1, (1888), pp.67-74.

Harrison, David, 'Freemasonry, Industry and Charity: The Local Community and the Working

Man', in *The Journal of the Institute of Volunteering Research,* Volume 5, Number 1, Winter, 2002, pp.33-45.

Harrison, David, 'Society in Flux' (co-authored with John Belton) in *The Journal for the Centre of Research into Freemasonry and Fraternalism*, Vol. 3, (University of Sheffield, 2010), pp.71-97.

Harrison, David, 'The Liverpool Masonic Rebellion and the Wigan Grand Lodge' in *The Transactions for the Historical Society for Lancashire and Cheshire*, Vol. 160, (University of Chester, 2011), pp.67-88.

Harrison, David, 'The Lymm Freemasons; A New Insight into Transition-Era Freemasonry', in *Heredom*, Vol. 19, (Washington: Scottish Rite Research Society, 2011), pp.169-190.

Sandbach, R.S.E., 'Robert Thomas Crucefix, 1788-1850', in *AQC,* Vol. 102, (1990), pp.134-163.

Warren, Charles, 'On the Orientation of Temples', in *AQC*, Vol. 1, (1888), pp.36-50.

Westcott, W.W., 'The Religion of Freemasonry illuminated by the Kabbalah', in *AQC*, Vol. 1, (1888), pp.55-59.

Wood, Douglas H., 'The Art of Memory and the Masonic Craft', in *Philalethes*, Vol. 65, No. 1, (2012), pp.6-15.

Woodford, A.F.A., 'Freemasonry and Hermeticisim', in *AQC*, Vol. 1, (1888), pp.28-36.

Articles

Article on Freemasons procession in Rugby, *Freemasonry Today*, No. 19, Grand Lodge Publications Ltd., (Autumn, 2012), p.24.

Gilbert, Robert A., 'Masonic Education: Leading the Way', in *MQ,*, Grand Lodge Publications, Issue 11, (October, 2004).

Harrison, David, 'The Masonic Rebellion in Liverpool and the Wigan Grand Lodge', *Freemasonry Today*, Issue 30, (October, 2004), pp.27-30.

Harrison, David, 'James Broadhurst and the Liverpool Masonic Rebellion', *MQ*, Grand Lodge Publications, Issue 13, (April, 2005), pp.34-36.

Harrison, David, 'The Grand Lodge of Wigan: Its Rise and Fall', *MQ*, Grand Lodge Publications, Issue 16, (January, 2006), pp.42-45.

Harrison, David, 'A Most Miserable Trade: Liverpool Freemasonry & Slavery', *Freemasonry Today*, Issue 39, (December, 2006), pp.36-38.

Harrison, David, 'Joseph Brant: A Masonic Legend', *MQ*, Grand Lodge Publications, Issue 23, (October 2007), pp.32-35.

Harrison, David, 'Secrecy and Suppression: Freemasonry and the Unlawful Society Act', *Freemasonry Today*, No. 2, (April, 2008), pp.26-28.

Harrison, David, 'Thomas Paine, Freemason?', *Freemasonry Today*, Issue 46, (Autumn 2008), pp.31-33.

Harrison, David, 'Freemasonry and the French Revolution', *Freemasonry Today*, Issue 49, (Summer 2009), pp.26-28.

Harrison, David, 'The American

Revolution', *Freemasonry Today*, Number 10, (Spring 2010), pp.43-45.

Harrison, David, 'Singapore and Freemasonry: The Life of Sir Stamford Raffles', *Freemasonry Today*, Number 11, (Summer 2010), pp.36-38.

Harrison, David, 'Edward Jenner', *Freemasonry Today*, Number 12, (Autumn 2010), pp.37-38.

Harrison, David, 'The Mystery of the Moving Coffins', *Freemasonry Today*, Number 13, (Winter 2010/11), pp.31-32.

Harrison, David, 'Authors' Lodge: A History', *Freemasonry Today*, Number 15, (Summer/Autumn 2011), pp.45-46.

Harrison, David, 'From Elias Ashmole to Arthur Edward Waite', *Philalethes*, Volume 64, No. 1, (Winter 2011), pp.21-29.

Harrison, David, 'James Ludovic Lindsay: Astronomer, Occultist and Freemason', *The Ashlar*, Issue 44, (September 2011), pp.36-37.

Harrison, David, 'Freemasonry, Occultists, and the Victorian Search for Hidden Knowledge', *The Square*, Volume 37, No. 4, (December 2011), pp.37-39.

Harrison, David, 'The Liverpool Masonic Rebellion and the Wigan Grand Lodge', *The Square*, Volume 38, No. 3, (September 2012), pp.6-10.

Harrison, David, 'Masonic Historians, their search for the origins of Freemasonry and the search for lost knowledge', *The Square*, Volume 39, No. 2, (June 2013), pp.11-14.

Lomax, Fred, "Fower Nowt One' – Royal Forest Lodge No. 401 and the Waddington Stone', *The Square*, September 2012, pp.22-23.

Marshall, George L., 'Brother Albert Pike's Duel', in *Knight Templar Magazine*, Vol. LVIII, No. 2, (February 2012), pp.10-13.

Websites

http://freemasonsfordummies.blogspot.co.uk/2011/08/grand-lodge-of-indiana-procession-last.html [accessed 25th of September, 2012]

http://www.grandlodgescotland.com/index.php?option=com_content&view=article&id=366:masonic-words-and-proper-names&catid=55:masonic-articles&Itemid=200 [accessed 31st of October, 2012]

http://www.masonicforumoflight.com/PDFS/ORDERSPDF.pdf [accessed 31st of October, 2012]

www.merseylodge5434.org/ [accessed 5th of October, 2012]

http://news.bbc.co.uk/1/hi/uk/politics/57381.stm [accessed 17th of October, 2012]

http://www.ugle.org.uk/how-to-become-a-mason/university-section/ [accessed 17th of October, 2012]

http://scottishrite.org/wp-content/uploads/2010/12/heredom_v17_rituals.pdf [accessed 5th of September, 2012]

K. Arrington, 'Highest Hills or Lowest Vales', www.masonicworld.com [accessed on 30th of December, 2012]

The history of the Mullan Pass Historic Lodge No. 1862 which presently meets on the historic site, see http://www.helenamasons.org/MullanPass05.htm [accessed on 30th of December, 2012]

The history of the Robert Burns Lodge No. 97 and the Malheur Cave, see http://www.burnslodge.org/malheur.html [accessed on 30th of December, 2012]

Barnes, Michael, 'Spoilt for Choice', *MQ*, Issue 10, (July, 2004), http://www.mqmagazine.co.uk/issue-10/p-62.php [accessed on 16th of January, 2012]

http://www.halcyontemple.org/about/ [accessed 15th of February, 2013]

Grand Lodge of Scotland (Founded 1736): http://www.grandlodgescotland.com

Grand Lodge of Western Australia: http://www.freemasonswa.org.au/

Grand Lodge South Australia & Northern Territory: http://www.santfreemasons.org.au/

Grand Lodge of Tasmania: http://www.freemasonrytasmania.org/

United Grand Lodge of Victoria: http://www.freemasonsvic.net.au/

United Grand Lodge of New South Wales & Australian Capital Territory: http://www.masons.org.au/

United Grand Lodge of Queensland: http://www.uglq.org.au/

United Grand Lodge of England (Founded 1717): http://www.ugle.org.uk